Taking The Narrative

Ashlee Frazier

Taking Back the Narrative

Published 2022

Printed in the United States of America

ISBN: **978-1-945423-45-1**

Cover Design: Aimee Brooks

Interior design by ILN staff

For information:

rjohnson@ilncenter.com

Publisher

International Localization Network

500 Westover Dr. #19552

Sanford, NC 27330

randy2905@gmail.com

Dedication

To my friends and family who have made this possible. There are too many people to name personally, so to everyone who has encouraged, empowered, loved, and stood by me as I fought to make this happen. I am eternally grateful. To everyone who read even just the smallest sections to give me feedback, to those who took my incessant calls every time an idea came to me. This has happened because of you.

To any student I have had the pleasure of knowing, whether through camp, retreat, youth or some other random way, this is for you. You were my inspiration and what kept me going when I wanted to quit.

Lastly, I would like to thank my bed. Where most of my ideas came to me when I was trying to fall asleep. This could not have happened without you.

Also to my parents and siblings who were mad I was going to single out my bed and not them. Mom, Dad, Kelsey and Austin.

Contents

Setting
the
Scene

Chapter One:

As the Story Goes

When Rachel was in 10th grade, she had everything she could have ever wanted in life. She had made the varsity swim team; she had amazing friends, and she was doing great in school. Most importantly, she loved God with her whole heart, soul, and mind. She was a fiery, powerful young lady who honestly did not care what people thought of her.

Towards the end of her sophomore year of high school, her friends noticed that one of the boys on the swim team, Bryan, had a crush on Rachel. Rachel immediately felt the Lord say she was not supposed to date this boy, but all of her friends thought they would be a cute couple. So after some convincing, she gave into the pressure and said yes to going on a date and they started dating. As they finished their sophomore year, she was still very hesitant about the relationship, but kept going because she enjoyed being around him. He was funny and loving, and after a few things happened in her life, she began to cling to him.

At first, their relationship was amazing. They had fun; they loved Jesus and, for what they thought was love at the time, they loved each other. As they continued dating, things came up that Rachel was not really prepared for. Things happened from a physical standpoint that had never been mentioned to her, and she felt very lost and confused. Rachel had amazing parents, but when you are sixteen and know everything, you don't ask your parents about some things, and to bring it up in church was never even a thought that crossed her mind. She believed that if she brought it up in church, she would be judged and people would start looking at her differently.

As she continued to date Bryan, she noticed she had not really been prepared for what being in a relationship was really like. Growing up, all she heard in school and in church was to "just say no" for basically anything. When it came to alcohol, drugs or sex, the answer was always to "just say no." Before this point in her life, she had never questioned that statement. She had no interest in drugs. Her parents had always let her try a bit of their alcohol when they were drinking, so she saw no point in drinking anywhere else. She had never dated anyone, so she thought saying no to sex would be easy.

However, no one prepared her for the fact that not only is sex something your body will crave, but there is more to sex than just the act itself. Which meant the first time he put his hand under her shirt, she did not know what to do or think about it. Or the next time when he put his hand down her pants, she was at a loss. No one had ever covered this part of a relationship with her. So as things escalated in her relationship, anxiety and guilt grew inside of her. As things escalated physically, she could feel parts of both of them changing. Where he once was very kind and loving, he became more impatient. Where she used to be confident, she became insecure.

They both began to change. Bryan started hanging out with a different group of friends and Rachel only wanted to hang out with him because hanging out with anyone else left her feeling guilty because of everything she was hiding and left a pit in her stomach. When she was seventeen, she lost her virginity to him. Although if you don't count technicalities, it had happened way before that. She would hear in a sermon later in life that somewhere around 70 percent of sexually active teenage girls end up struggling with depression. She fell into that statistic.

Suddenly, she was acting differently. Things she used to enjoy no longer seemed worth doing. While her anxiety grew, she thought maybe she could start feeling better about herself if she was with Bryan or knew for sure what he thought about her. All of this time, Rachel continued to notice things in her personality changing. Where she used to be more carefree and loving, she was becoming jealous and less confident. Where she used to love thinking about her future, she hated the idea of it. Everything in her life seemed less bright.

Things that usually would roll right off of her shoulders seemed to sit on them with extra weight. Not things that deserved weight, but in the same sense that when you are hangry, your emotions seem heightened and things that usually aren't a big deal become a major deal. That was what she was feeling. Things that shouldn't have bothered her were bothering her. For instance, if her friends made a joke, all the sudden it would feel like they hated her. Even though she herself was very sarcastic and had always been able to take jokes, everything was feeling dark. She could not understand why these feelings kept coming up.

What she knew was when she was with that boy, things seemed better. At least for a little while. Rachel had become so lost that she let more and more things slide by in her relationship. She had forgotten she was a confident, independent person, and she was feeling like she had to do whatever he asked to make him happy. She forgot whom her identity should be in and started searching to find it in Bryan.

Instead of breaking up with him the first time she found out he had feelings for someone else, her immediate thought was, "what is wrong with me?" She felt lost. So she kept on sleeping with Bryan to feel good about herself for a second, then to go home feeling guilty. She kept putting up with small comments like "one of my friends noticed you had love handles the other day" and assumed she was fat and unattractive even though she wasn't. She lost who she was.

One day, while sitting in her car, she had a fight with Bryan about him telling another girl he had feelings for her. She could not understand how she had fallen this far. How the girl that used to be filled with fire and confidence was left bawling in her car alone about a boy who couldn't see her worth. As Bryan got less caring, Rachel got more insecure, which caused her to become more dramatic. As Rachel became more dramatic and jealous, Bryan continued to push her away. Neither one of them was who they started as. They both made so many mistakes.

As most relationships go, it is rarely one person or the other who causes a problem. Most of the time, it's both. In the summer of Rachel's senior year, she noticed how far she had fallen. How far she was from the girl she used to know who was brave, fierce, and filled with love for people. She would have so many moments where she felt so empowered after a mission trip or camp and would be ready to end the relationship, only to have the exact right words said to her when she got home.

One night, at an absolute low in her life, she was hanging out with Bryan and some of his friends. He was in the pool and she was sitting on the deck, so Bryan asked her to text his mom from his phone to ask her a question. When she pulled up the text messages, she saw a text thread from him and his two best friends. The last text told her something was off and so she let her curiosity get the best of her. That text thread held a conversation where he told his friends he had feelings for another girl and he was considering trying to make a move on her. At that moment, her heart sank.

Being someone who hated causing a scene, she texted his mom like he asked, went inside and cried her eyes out, wondering "why am I not enough?" Rachels' one saving grace from that night was the fact that one of Bryans' friends came to Rachel's defense and told him she would not discuss anything of that matter while he was still dating Rachel. Rachel would find out later in life that he did try to make a move on that girl, which she had always suspected. After that night, all Rachel could think about was how she wanted out of the relationship but didn't know how to do it.

She had given everything she was to him and didn't understand the power of Christ's forgiveness. She was trapped between feeling like she would disappoint Christ and everyone around her if she left the relationship. She felt worthless and that no one would love somebody who had been "damaged."

Finally, in the month before she went to college, Bryan told her he wanted to go on a break for the first month of school. He told her he thought it would be best if they did college separately (but she couldn't see anyone) and then come back together.

It was finally at that moment Rachel remembered she was worth something. As she sat in her truck waiting for him to come out so they could have this conversation, she heard the Lord say to her, "Beloved, why do you think you have no worth?" Having grown up in church, she gave a nice Sunday school answer. "Of course I know I am worth something!" Immediately she heard the Lord say, "then why aren't you acting like it?"

It was the first time she had really heard the Lord's voice since dating Bryan. Not that God wasn't speaking to her; it was merely that she hadn't been listening. So when Bryan got in the car and asked how she felt about the break, she said she wouldn't do it. That she did not deserve to be treated as something he could put to the side until he decided if he wanted it in college or not. And they broke up.

On the drive home, she made a promise to the Lord. She promised she would not get into a relationship without His permission ever again. She would wait for the okay from Him, and He promised that in His time, He would send someone to her.

As Rachel started college, she remembered how much fun her life used to be. She remembered little things about herself and got back some of the fire that had been so burnt out. She would struggle with anxiety for a few more years, but mostly, she was thriving. Even through the midst of her anxiety, she had an amazing amount of new encounters with God and continued to learn more about who God was and who she was.

She went into college with a major in Electronic Media and Communications. She didn't really want to do that, but she felt like she needed to decide what to do with her life. While she was in college, she would work through all of her emotions on what happened in her relationship and eventually would come to forgive herself and find a new wholeness in Christ.

During the summer of her freshman year, she interned with a Christian non-profit helping with their video editing. Within the first week of being there, she knew it was not what she wanted to do in life. She loved the non-profit and the people she was with, but she found no joy in what she was there to do. She kept the internship, but continuously wondered what she was supposed to do with her life.

About a month into her internship, she got a call from her mom informing her that one of her childhood friends had committed suicide. It was a pain she had never felt before, but within that pain, she felt a newfound comfort. It was one of the first moments in her life she could feel the comfort of the Holy Spirit. In that moment of heartbreak, she began praying that God would show her what she was meant to do. Rachel knew there had to be more to life than what she was currently doing. She knew she had a heart for helping people and wanted to pour into people's lives to be able to help those who were struggling.

She added a second degree in Human Sciences to her program so she could learn more about what it looks like helping people who struggle with depression and anxiety. While that was a step in the right direction, she still felt there was something more for her, so she continued fervently praying for the three months of her internship that the Lord would open her eyes to what she was called to do.

After three months of praying, she returned home for the start of the new school year. The first Sunday she was home, her church announced that their current youth ministry intern was leaving. When she heard, she felt in her gut she should apply for the internship, but ignored it because she did not want to go into ministry. A few days later, she was talking to her old youth pastor, and he made a joke about her wanting to be involved in every ministry except his. Without realizing the words coming out of her mouth, she said, "I never said I wasn't interested." (that was a lie. She had indeed said she did not want to work in the youth ministry.) That conversation led to an interview which led to her getting the job, which led to her feeling a call to ministry.

She was unsure what part of ministry she wanted to go into, but knew she loved working with her students. Her life was transformed during her time in youth ministry. It's where she felt the call to full-time ministry. Where she found out she was capable of so much more than she realized, and where she got the opportunity to do life with some amazing students - some of whom would end up being her best friends. During her time in youth ministry, she preached for the first time and felt a small urge in her to keep doing it. An urge she ignored because she hated public speaking. She never imagined it would turn into anything more than teaching at her youth group, but she had some small feeling it might be something more.

During this time in youth ministry, intermixed with her college classes; she looked back at her relationship to try to figure out what caused things to go so wrong. She wondered why she made certain decisions and why in some moments she had acted so irrationally and attention seeking when that is not who she was. She had grown up in a magnificent home, had a phenomenal community and a life-giving church. None of which taught her to act like that.

As she sat in one of her classes, she realized it was not any of the people in her life who taught her those things. Rather, the people she saw on her screens. It was the dramas she watched that said being dramatic will get your boy to do something romantic. It was the shows and movies she watched that gave her these ideas of how to get attention. Again, they both made mistakes in that relationship, so there was more to her reactions, but there was also a sizable chunk of things that could be traced back to the shows she watched.

As her time went on, she continued to ponder these things. In her senior year of college, she felt the Lord call her to a ministry school in California. During her first year at that school she had more people than she would have liked come up to her and tell her they felt the Lord saying she was "a torch bearer", "a leader among leaders", "a trailblazer", "someone who was meant to preach on a stage." Every time she got words like that, she wanted it less and less, but she heard it from so many people in different environments she did not feel as though she could ignore it.

About two months into school, she had a powerful encounter with God, when He set her free from anxiety. From there, she realized the thing holding her back from everything that had been spoken over her was fear. This fear kept her from pursuing the path she felt the Lord speaking over her life. In that same encounter with God, she was set free from her fear of public speaking and felt the call on her life to preach. As the year continued, she got a better picture of the Lord's call on her life. When she finally felt she recognized what God was asking of her, a bigger wrench got thrown in. She felt a call to write a book. A thought that had never once been in her mind.

Three days later, a fellow student who she had never met before came up and told her she felt like God was saying Rachel was called to write a book. The Lord had been reminding her of all of those thoughts she had in college, trying to analyze why her relationship and high school life had been so draining and felt the Lord say it was time to share that information with the world. She started to realize that all of those things she had experienced, the insecurities, the unawareness, the pain, were being felt by so many other people. Other people needed to know that there is hope. There is light. There is redemption.

This may not be the most dramatic story. It doesn't have all the crazy twists and turns of a show you would watch today. It isn't filled with unrealistic romance or teen defiance or any of the other things that make teen dramas so intriguing to watch. But this, this is my story.

Chapter Two:

The Golden Media

In our time and culture, it is very hard to go even a single day without using some form of media. I don't believe media is bad, but I believe the way we view it could be problematic. Not only that, but I believe it is affecting our lives in ways that we do not see. Just like in my story in the previous chapter, I had no idea that the shows I was watching were having that deep of an impact in my life. In the coming chapters, I will discuss more specifically how these shows were affecting me, but first we need to understand why it is important to recognize how we view the media.

In Exodus 32, we see the story of the golden calf. I encourage you to go read the story, but here is a review. God had just brought the Israelites out of Egypt when He invited Moses to the top of a mountain to talk. While Moses was on the mountain, the Israelites were left waiting for Moses to return. After a while, they grew impatient and decided they wanted a new god to worship. Aaron, Moses' brother, took all the gold jewelry from the people and created a golden calf that the people worshiped and sacrificed to. On the mountain, God told Moses of what was happening with His people and told Moses He was going to unleash His wrath upon them. Moses begged the Lord to change His mind and succeeded. When Moses went back down the mountain, he carried two tablets in his hand that were the writings of God. When Moses got to the Israelites' camp, he became enraged and threw the tablets down. He divided the camp and told them whoever is on the Lord's side should come to him and they killed the people who had turned against God.

I used to read the story of the golden calf and would laugh to myself and think, "Thank goodness we are not like that anymore!" To the past me and to those of you who may be caught in the same mindset, while we may not worship a golden calf anymore, we are far from being free from the worship of idols. We just evolved. They worshiped with a golden calf in the middle; we worship the thing in the middle of most of our living rooms.

Now catch this. In the story, the golden calf itself was not bad. It was the way they treated it that caused it to become an idol. The same goes for the media. I do not believe by itself it is bad, but the way we treat it is. We look at cavemen and judge them for being so entranced by a little flickering light (fire), but are we really so different? The changing light still fascinates us. It's just more advanced now.

The fact that most of our free time is spent on some form of media, be it television, movies, news, social, etc., causes it to become a false idol. It took me a long time to admit to myself that I tend to idolize TV more than I worship the King. It was hard for me to recognize because I know who my creator is and I have always loved God for as long as I can remember. However, my actions would not show the same thing.

My actions would show I loved my Netflix account more than I loved Jesus. Why? Because we spend time with the things we love most. If I looked at what I was spending the most time with, the answer was not Jesus. I am not saying this to bring shame, but to bring light to the fact that just because we do not stand in a circle singing chants to something does not mean we do not worship it.

Unrealistic? Inconvenient?

One reason I think we struggle with a lifestyle of worship is because we feel like we have to fit worship into our lives when, in reality, our lives need to fit into worship. I used to think to myself that reading my Bible every day or worshiping every day was unrealistic. A thought I know many others have also had. Over the years, I think we have confused the meanings of unrealistic and inconvenient. Finding time to worship every day isn't unrealistic. It's inconvenient for how I currently live my life. It's inconvenient to read my Bible. It is not unrealistic.

Even if you have a jam-packed day, you can worship on your way to work, you can read your Bible while you're on the toilet, you can find time. Why? Because we make time for the things we care about. According to the Bureau of Labor and Statistics (2016), the average American spends around three hours of leisure time watching television. In another study it showed that on average, Americans spend about five hours a day on leisure activities and less than thirty minutes on religious activities. I think one reason we tend to spend so much less time with God is because we have been taught the way you are "supposed" to do it. We were taught how you are "supposed" to spend time with God, and created a mindset that says there are only certain ways to connect with God, and not doing the exact thing someone tells you, means you are a "bad Christian." I believe this has caused us to detest that time. We were taught to value a routine over a relationship, and if your routine did not look a certain way, then you were not disciplined enough.

The biggest advice I give to students and friends is to find the way you connect with Jesus most and put that in your schedule every day. I have heard many devotionals in my life about making sure to get your Bible reading time in, as well as a devotional, as well as some journaling and so on and so forth. I would get overwhelmed with how much I was "supposed" to do that I did none of it, and would use the excuse that it was an unrealistic expectation to expect me to do all of those things. I would end up feeling so much shame about the fact that I was not doing the "right thing."

We can learn from Jesus' life and conversations with the Pharisees that just knowing scripture is not enough. It is about relationships. When you read the Bible, but you only do it from obligation and don't learn from it or let it transform you, then you are not truly living in a relationship. In order to be transformed by scripture, we have to read it from a place of love, not performance. In order to learn from the Bible, you need to be in love with the one who wrote it. I for years would read the Bible and would get nothing out of it, so I would stop reading it. It wasn't until I was given the advice to do what I personally feel the deepest connection with the Lord in that I learned more about who God was and felt a deeper connection with Him that carried into my daily routine. From there, I grew deeper and deeper in love with Jesus.

From that love and relationship grew a want to read my Bible, a want to listen to sermons and have discussions about the Bible, but the first step was falling in love. I realized reading my Bible once a day was not unrealistic, because it takes five minutes to read a chapter. The more you care for something, the more time you will make time for it. It doesn't need to be what society says a perfect Christian life looks like, it just needs to look like a relationship.

In the same way that every marriage looks different, every relationship with Christ looks different. What might work for you to connect with God probably looks very different from others. What works for me, may not work for other people in my life. For me, I found that if I start my day with worship, the rest of my day looks different. I then have more of a want to be in scripture, prayer and conversations.

Once I stopped doing what I felt I had to do, I started noticing the change it made in my life. It was easier to spend more time with Jesus because I started my day in connection with Him. I realized that the more I worked on relationships, the easier it was to spend less time on a screen. Not to say that I do not still struggle some days, but it became more of a priority in my life to have intentional time with God. I in no way want to tell anyone to stop using the media all together. That would be very hypocritical of me. My only goal is to help people recognize the role it plays in their life.

When the Israelites were worshiping the golden calf, the calf itself was not the issue. Their mindset towards the calf was the issue. If I got a little golden calf and put it on my desk, that would not be a sin. The calf became sin when they worshiped and sacrificed to it. I recognize in our time we don't do burnt sacrifices, but we do still make sacrifices. So the crucial question we have to look at is, how does the story of the Israelites compare to our time?

What are we sacrificing?

One of the easiest ways to tell if something has become an idol is to check what you are making sacrifices for. In the old testament, the Israelites make sacrifices of things God had given them to show their thanks. For example, they would give an animal or some of their crop, things they found most precious.

Today, our values are a little different. I would say two of the things we find most precious are time and money. So the question becomes, where are you sacrificing those two things? We say time is precious and yet can spend hours sacrificing precious time on things like TikTok (I am as guilty of this as anyone.) Personally, I always feel like I do not have enough time to do the things I want. Whether that's travel, writing, hanging out with people, life always seems a little hectic. But truth be told, when I look at the breakdown of my days, I notice I spend a lot of time on things like TikTok, Netflix, Hulu, etc. I choose to sacrifice some of my time for those things constantly.

Again, I want to reiterate that none of those things in and of themselves are sinful (depending on what you are watching.) It becomes a problem when they hold a higher place in our lives than God. You can tell where they each rank by what you sacrifice to them. When it comes to money, are you willing to spend significant amounts of money a month on various streaming services? If you felt a push on your heart to put that same amount into the church or into others, would you feel the same? For me it was watching TV shows, and I won't lie to you and tell you that it's not a struggle still, because it is. For you, it could be something totally different. It could be video games, work, social media, football, really anything can make its way to being an idol.

I encourage you, over the next few weeks, to take an honest look into your life and ask yourself, what things do I make sacrifices for? How much of my time and money are spent on these things while when it comes to God, I claim I just do not have time to fit all of those things into my schedule. For me, this was a real eye-opener as to how I was spending my time. Once I realized it wasn't actually unrealistic, it was just inconvenient, my life changed.

Have you lost your patience?

One thing that I think is vital to recognize in this passage is why the Israelites turned against God. The people in Israel did not turn against God because they believed Him to be evil or out of anger. They created an idol purely because they were tired of waiting for God. They grew anxious and were ready to move on with their lives, which caused them to create an idol.

When I stop to think about it, I do the same thing in my life all the time. If the Lord is taking more time than I would like, I look to myself or other things to get them done because

I am impatient. I believe we see that a lot in our world today. We ask God to move in our lives, but stop praying because we are tired of waiting and decide to find a worldly, temporary fix. We ask for a move but grow tired of searching. Or we use the excuse that we are tired and need to spend some time "resting" watching television or being on social media.

I believe that impatience is a major reason we do not see some of our prayers answered. NF is currently my favorite rapper. In his song "Oh Lord" he makes the statement, "It's hard to answer prayers when nobody's praying to you." If you haven't heard this song, I encourage you to stop right now and go listen to it. A lot of what he says fits into what I will be talking about throughout the book.

We get caught in this cycle, just like the Israelites. We can see God move powerfully and set us free, but if His next act doesn't come in the timing we want, we doubt His goodness. There are a lot of times when I read the Bible and I come across stories like the Israelites or so many others in scripture where they see God move in powerful ways, and it seems like they immediately forget what God did for them. When I used to read these, I would always think, "How is that even plausible? How could you forget God split a sea for you? How could you forget all the miracles you have seen and switch to worshiping a false god? How could you so quickly move past what God has done?"

One day when I was reading and asking these questions I felt the Lord say, "that's a good question, Ashlee. How can you forget so easily?" I quickly realized I could answer my question. I could understand how they could so quickly forget because I do that all the time. For me, it just looks a little different. Instead of parting the waters, the questions would go more like this. How could you forget God has freed you from anxiety? How could you forget that you have seen miracles that your eyes and brain cannot comprehend? How could you forget all the ways God has come through in your life? The answer is simple. We choose to focus on what is directly in front of us, instead of remembering how God has come through in our past.

When I look at my past, I am even more convinced that God will come through in every aspect of my future because He has already done so time and time again. So often we get caught in the same circle that the Israelites did. Seeing a miracle, then doubting God. Seeing a miracle, then moving on to something else. For us, instead of moving to worship around a calf, we grow impatient and try to fill our needs with something temporary. We turn on the television to temporarily forget the stresses of work or school or relationships instead of having the patience to wait for God to come through.

Until we stop idolizing the things of the world, we won't see the outpouring of God that we all so desperately post about on social media. One day, while I was scrolling through social media, I saw a person post about how this land needs Jesus (we do.) As I read it, I heard the Lord say to me, "would you even see it if a move happened?" and I wondered to myself. If a move of God happened, would I notice? What do I know about the moves of God that are happening? Because trust me, He is on the move, even if we do not see it or know about it. Or the better question, if a move of God was happening, would I even believe it? Or would I count it as false because it doesn't line up exactly with my theology?

I really hope not. I hope I am attuned enough with the Lord to recognize when He is on the move, but I also know there have been times in my life where I have missed a move because I was too busy doing basically anything else. It is so important to recognize your beliefs and convictions, but it is just as important to recognize that sometimes we are wrong. If we want to see a move of God, it may just mean that we need to look up from our screens.

Chapter Three:

The Outside In

Growing up, I was always a little less emotional than everyone around me. Things just never seemed to faze me. I wasn't emotionless, but I definitely did not experience emotions as strongly as those around me. Situations would happen where everyone would be in tears and I would be sad, but not in tears. Honestly, that became a part of my life I would pride myself on. I would take pride in the fact I could take on anything and be okay.

As I got older, some of those things changed. Things started hitting me differently. I felt things a lot more strongly, but had this perception of myself saying I needed to be the strong one. What I realized is what they could see as a lack of emotion was just a difference in emotion. Instead of feeling sad, I would feel frustrated or worried. Instead of crying, my brain would immediately go to how do I fix this, or how do I help those around me. My emotions looked different, and I never understood that. It has taken me years to obtain a better understanding of my emotions.

I have heard many sermons in my life about emotions, and the majority of those were from someone who struggled to control their emotions, which was something I could only relate to a little. I rarely have heard messages about what it looks like being in touch with your emotions so that you can experience additional aspects of God. In order to have control over our emotions, we have to recognize that we have them.

The first time I started writing about this, I was creating a seminar for a middle school camp. Going into it, I didn't realize the impact it would have. I went into it expecting kids would learn a little, but in no way did I expect kids to get emotional during the seminar. Without fail, every time I did the seminar, there would be a student who left the seminar in tears. On the second day I gave the seminar, I spotted one girl in particular in the middle of the room who, from the first second I shared a bit of my testimony of how I came to learn to use my emotions, was crying. I was very confused because nothing in my seminar was emotional; it was just teaching on what it looks like living life aware of your emotions. It distracted me the whole time, trying to figure out why this girl was crying, wondering if it was something unrelated to what I was talking about or if something I had said had struck a chord with her.

She left the seminar before I had the chance to talk to her, so I went to the Lord in prayer to pray for this girl and as I did, I heard Him clearly say "She was crying because that was the first time someone in the church told her that her emotions matter." I was shocked because I honestly hadn't thought of this seminar as a ground-breaking thing. My purpose had always been to just help these middle schoolers have a better understanding of their emotions before they created bad habits emotionally.

I doubted a bit that I had actually heard the Lord correctly, because I was struggling to believe my seminar could be the reason she had been crying. Later that night, I was talking with one of my good friends about how his small group had gone and he proceeded to tell me about one girl in his small group who had gone to my seminar. He said this girl from the moment I started speaking could not stop crying and left the seminar still in tears. I stood there in disbelief that this girl would be in one of my best friends' small groups, but I waited in silence for him to continue. He went on to say that she told the small group her entire life she had been told to ignore her emotions. That her emotions had no importance. But, during my seminar, she felt for the first time in her life her feelings and emotions had value.

It was at that moment I realized how important this conversation is. How crucial it is to discuss the importance of using emotions to help in discernment and the importance for people like me, who have struggled with feeling they are not emotional enough to also share their stories and how they connect with the world. Emotions were never meant for us to ignore them. They were given to us for a purpose.

Using media to feel things

Sometimes in life, we decide that instead of actually dealing with our own emotions, we will use a show, movie or social media to feel those same things. For example, if you are feeling sad and feel as though you need to cry, you may watch a sad movie to make yourself cry. Or maybe you watch a sitcom when you are angry so that you can laugh and boost your mood. That way you can get out those emotions without actually dealing with how you are feeling. We also have a bad habit of using social media to get immediate gratification for insecurities instead of trying to find the root of the problem. All of these are a temporary fix. A fix that momentarily makes it feel as though you have dealt with the things you need to, when in reality you just put a bandaid over a cut that needs stitches. In order to actually deal with emotions, we need to address what is causing them, not distract ourselves with something that is a little bit easier. Watching a show or using social media to get our emotions out is kind of like drinking soda on a hot day. It may cool you off, but it will not hydrate you.

Why are emotions important?

God gave us emotions for a reason. Like everything else He created, our emotions are beautiful, meaningful, and purposeful. I believe sometimes, as Christians, we get this idea that we need to ignore our emotions because they are not always trustworthy, but I propose our emotions were given to us to help, not to hinder. They were given to us to help us discern things and to learn from and to experience additional aspects of who Christ is. They were never meant to be bottled up. There is a balance that is needed with emotions, because we never want them to be the only thing we make decisions off of, but they are a precious tool.

In order to understand the importance of emotions, we must first have a little understanding of emotions. If you have never seen the movie Inside Out', I highly recommend watching it in order to understand how each emotion is important. The only thing I would do differently is change Joy's name to Happiness, because joy differs greatly from happiness. Which is another thing that is vital to understand when looking at the importance of our emotions. Happiness is a feeling. It is fleeting; it comes and goes as it pleases. People can take it from you. People can give it to you. Joy is a fruit of the spirit. It can be felt in all aspects of emotion and life. As you spend more time with Jesus, you find more joy. If you watch Inside Out, I would say at the beginning of the movie, joy is purely based on happiness. At the end of the movie, she is transformed into joy. In the end, you can see joy becoming a part of every emotion. She is not confined to herself, but instead is used in sadness, fear, anger and disgust.

This is important to recognize because you can feel joy in every emotion. Joy can be a part of anger, sadness, and worry. Happiness is not. Happiness is always based on circumstance. For instance, if someone gives you a gift card to your favorite restaurant, you feel happiness. If someone came up and stole the gift card from you, you would feel sad. Which is the difference between joy and happiness. Joy is found as you grow closer to the Lord. Happiness is found in people, shows, social media, or things of the world. Happiness grows and fades with circumstances. For a little more reference, I created a table to make it a little easier to understand.

Joy	Happiness
Sustainable strength	Fickle feeling
Internal source	External source
Fruit of the Spirit	Temporary
Can be experienced in any emotion	Can be snatched away by circumstances
Supernatural	Worldly

As for the rest of the emotions, I believe it is important to recognize that none of the emotions are any more important than the rest, and trying to only stay in one emotion causes more problems, such as anxiety, depression or toxic positivity. As people, we each have an emotion we lean into the most. This emotion is usually our first response when a circumstance comes up.

Take, for example, the following situation.

It's the weekend and you see a bunch of your friends decided to hang out, but they did not invite you. Which response is closest to how you would react?

    A. Immediately become sad and spend the night watching sad movies

B. Get pissed off and call your friends to give them a piece of your mind

C. Begin wondering what you did wrong, and think they must all hate you for something you did.

D. Give them the benefit of the doubt and choose to believe there is an explanation for why you were not invited.

Or another example

Someone close to you dies suddenly, do you...

A. Take the time to mourn for a couple of days

B. Angrily ask God why He took them away from you

C. Immediately worry about how you need to be helping others get through this.

D. Reminisce over the time you had with them and be thankful you got to know them.

In any of these situations, there is not an answer that is more right. They are just responses from different people. When I gave this seminar at camp, I had the students stand up and go to the corners of the room that matched the response they would have and gave them a few more circumstances. One thing I observed most was it always shocked them that not everyone answered the same as they did. Everyone handles life differently, and I believe it is important to recognize your tendency for response in order to grow into a mature, well-rounded person who lets their emotions have a part of their life without letting them control them.

It is also important to recognize that just because you experience sadness or anger, that does not mean you are not fun to be around. It just means you handle life differently. For me, my immediate emotion is usually frustration. I want to understand why something is a certain way or figure out how I can fix it. I would be bold enough to say that no one in my life considers me an angry person. It is just my immediate response to bad situations.

Sometimes sadness and anger get a bad rap. We believe that they are emotions we should not feel, but in reality they are just as important as joy and sadness, and are dangerous to avoid. When you avoid any of your emotions, you end up bottling them up until they end up exploding.

Toxic Positivity

One extremely important thing to recognize while reading this is that toxic positivity can be just as detrimental as depression, anxiety or anger issues. Here is what it is not. It is not being an optimistic person. The easiest way I could describe toxic positivity is that it is when you refuse to recognize that any other emotions exist at all. There will be times in our life where we have moments of anger, doubt and sadness. Refusing to recognize those in ourselves and others is an unhealthy response.

The beauty in negative emotions

One of the things that has taken me so long to understand is the idea that negative emotions are not only significant, but essential in creating a deeper intimacy. Think about it. In a marriage, if you push down sadness and anger any time they arise, you will be led to a very hateful place. However, when you let the emotions show and work through them together, you develop a deeper intimacy. There is a reason we were given more emotions than just happiness. If we were only meant to be happy, then we would not have been given a full scale of emotions. But since we were given multiple emotions, I have to believe that there is a reason for it. They are there to be a useful tool for us.

When we think of emotions such as anger and sadness, we often think that they are emotions we are not meant to dwell on. Emotions that when we feel them we need to suppress them and pretend that we aren't really feeling anything but happiness. But if we were only ever meant to feel happiness, then why do all the other emotions exist?

I have always heard people say "It is okay to not be okay." But for me, this is a concept that I truly struggle to make a part of my life. Being okay is something I pride myself in. When I start to find myself struggling, my immediate thought is never to go to someone. It is to figure out why I am feeling that way, and work it out on my own. Part of that comes from being very independent, but the far greater majority can be boiled down to one thing: fear. Fear that people will see me as weak. Fear that people won't see my problems as "real." Fear that people will not care.

As I was writing this book, I came upon a time where I was inexplicably sad. I had nothing going on in my life to make me sad, but everyday I woke up something just felt off. Since I had nothing that I could point to for a reason, I tried to brush it off and pretend that everything was okay even though it felt as though my life was anywhere except where I wanted it to be. As I was reading back through the section you are reading now, I couldn't help but feel guilty. Who was I to write on emotions when I was not currently living fully into what I had written. The truth is, it is a daily struggle for me to remind myself that my emotions have a part in my everyday life.

It was then that I started to realize that maybe, just maybe, this struggle was exactly why I needed to write this. For the other people, who are like me, and struggle to let their emotions live in their life. For those who need help to navigate their emotions. In all honesty, finding beauty in negative emotions is still a huge struggle for me. I have to constantly remind myself that there are purposes for my emotions and I do not have to understand them. In those times where I have let those emotions in, those are the moments where I felt intimacy with God that I never imagined, because it was then when I let Him into the good, the bad, and the ugly,

How do we see this in scripture?

One reason I think my generation stopped reading scripture as much is because we read it without emotion, but these stories were *real people* who had genuine emotions the same way you and I experience them. I am going to share with you the two things I do in order to help me recognize the role emotions play throughout scripture.

The first is that I started watching *The Chosen. The Chosen* is a beautiful TV series that follows the life of Christ but shows it in a new way. It goes through the stories of the other characters we see in scripture and does a beautiful job of making stories I have heard my whole life come to life. This is a great way to fall back in love with scripture. Watching TV is something most of us have already cut time out of our schedule for. This is just switching what you watch every once in a while.

The second thing I started doing was walking through the stories I was reading with an activity to point out characters' emotions. I will show an example of this with the story of Lazarus being raised from the dead.

Step one: Read the passage

Step two: Go through the passage again, but imagine yourself in it. What would you be feeling?

Step three: Write out the emotions

Who in this passage showed sadness?

Who showed anger?

Who showed worry?

Who was happy?

Example: Lazarus rising from the dead.

Step one: Read the story (John 11)

Step two: How would you feel?

If I was in this situation, I can only imagine that my emotions would feel a bit like a tornado. I would be incredibly sad, stressed, frustrated and eventually happy. If I were a disciple, I would have mostly been worried and frustrated because I would have been wondering why we weren't going to heal our friend, but I would also be worried about the fact that the last time we were in that city, people threatened to kill us.

If I was Mary or Martha, I would have been pretty mad Jesus had not come. I would have been so angry that I knew someone who could have prevented my brother from dying but hadn't I also would have felt an immense amount of happiness.

Step three: Who showed emotions?

Sadness: everyone in the story

Happiness: everyone at the end

Worry: the disciples, Mary and Martha.

Anger/frustration: Thomas, in verse 16, was very pessimistic about the fact that they were going back to a town that threatened to kill them. Martha also seemed frustrated that Jesus had not come. I also think based on some of Jesus' responses, that Jesus may have been a little frustrated with the fact that everyone in this story had seen Him do miracles but they still doubted.

It is important for us to recognize the part our emotions play in our lives, so when we go into things like friendships or relationships, we understand what is at play within us. I think it is especially important to understand how we see emotions in scripture because we constantly see unstable emotions through television shows and social media.

Our emotions are a part of our everyday life. If we learn to utilize them, they can bring so much joy to our life, which is why it is important to understand them before I get into the rest of what I want to talk about. Our emotions impact our relationships, our work, our friends, the list goes on and on. The key question is, what is the importance of emotions in what I am talking about? The primary importance is that we understand emotions helps us create intimacy.

I expect one reason we tend to not show as many emotions in today's culture is because we are taught on some level to push down emotions, but I also believe that a bigger reason we chose to ignore them is because we have so many distractions that can keep us from recognizing what is actually going on in our lives. We can turn to social media, television shows, YouTube, movies, etc. These cause us to stop feeling the emotions, but they are only a temporary solution to feel better. It's easier to go to the media than to our friends, but that is a temporary solution. Eventually those feelings will come back. So the real question is: how do we use our emotions and why is it important?

Emotions create intimacy

In later chapters, I will cover this topic a little deeper, but for now, it is important to know a little of how emotions can affect a relationship. The reason I wanted to talk about emotions before getting into everything else is because we need to recognize the part they play in our relationships. I believe one reason there are shows like *Friends*, *The Office*, *New Girl* and *Parks and Recreation*, and other shows people continuously watch even though they have seen them so many times comes down to one main reason. We crave the relationships we see in those shows. We love the idea of having five or six friends we see all the time. Friends that are the first people you call when something happens. Friends who know every part of you, yet a lot of us struggle to find relationships like that.

I believe the biggest reason is because we are not willing to bring ourselves fully into the relationship in the way the people on those shows do. We hate letting people see us when we are at our lowest, so how can we expect a friend group to come around us if we do not give them the opportunity. We have this idea that if someone really wanted to know what was going on, then they would ask. Well, not just ask, they would ask, and we would say no. Then somehow they would just know something is going on and so they would keep probing and probing until finally we break down and answer the question. At least that's what we want, right?

Unfortunately, that rarely happens. We claim "no one ever asks" but yet we get asked how we are doing multiple times a day. It's on us to choose to not tell the truth. Hear me out. I am not saying that when any random person asks you how you are doing, you should give them your life story. I am saying our friends and family ask us this question constantly, just as we ask it to others. It is so much easier for us to blame it on the other person than to admit that maybe it's because of our own actions that we feel like we are alone.

In high school and college, I struggled with anxiety. No one else knew about it. I would go out and put on my happy, excited face, but all the while be filled with anxiety. During that time was when I would put the blame on everyone but myself. I would think about the exact things I just talked about. "If they really knew me, they would know something is off." Or maybe you are just a wonderful actor. Or maybe that's been the only side of you they have seen, so how could they know the difference?

At this time in my life, I had a ridiculous amount of people who would have happily walked through that journey with me, but the one I want to focus on is my old youth pastor, who at the time was my boss. As I said earlier, I interned for my old youth group for three years in college. Those three years happened to be right in the middle of me dealing with anxiety. My youth pastor's name is Michael, and he is one of the most amazing people I have ever met. While in this internship we would meet weekly and every week he would ask "How are you doing?" and the rules were you could not answer with good, bad or okay. It could only be one word, so you had to come up with a more creative word to express exactly what you were feeling. After we gave our word, we could then explain why we chose that word. This gave me the perfect opportunity weekly to talk about some things I was struggling with. But I never did. I was held back by a fear that people either wouldn't care or would tell me what I was feeling was not real. It would be very easy for me to look at that time and blame it on Michael. To say that it was Michael's fault. To push the blame to someone other than myself, but the truth is, it was one hundred percent on me.

I knew his personality. I knew how big of a heart he has and how much he loves to help people, but I stayed silent. Had he known, I have no doubt in my mind he would have helped me. He helped me in ways I didn't realize at the time because of the way he lives his life and his life is covered in Jesus, but had I come to him and told him what was going on, he would have been able to help me in the way I needed. I don't know for sure, but I would bet good money that the first time I gave the testimony of my anxiety, he was probably a little hurt by the fact that I did not come to him.

The point is, I chose to stay in that spot of anxiety. I had people like Michael who loved me, but anxiety and fear do a funny thing of making you feel like everyone is against you and that you are alone. Had I gone to any of the people in my life a lot sooner, I can guarantee I would have been freed from anxiety a lot sooner.

Emotions create intimacy. But we need to be brave enough to bring those emotions to the table. Once I started bringing my emotions to the table, my relationships were transformed. That also opened the door for those around me to bring their emotions to the table. Only then did I experience the intimacy I had always craved.

Intimacy with the Father

Emotions create intimacy not only with people, but with Christ. Growing up, I always thought that in my relationship with Christ, I needed to be happy. I felt like if I wasn't happy, then it meant I did not trust in what God had planned for me. My second year of ministry school, that belief was completely flipped upside down.

When I entered the second year of ministry school, COVID had been running rampant for about 6 months. My life, as well as probably every single person reading this, got flipped upside down. All of a sudden, I had gone from a thriving community to spending most of my time alone. I went from being active and doing all kinds of things to bringing Netflix in bed most of the day. I was mad, sad, frustrated, worried; I was feeling all the emotions except happiness. Yet every time I would pray, I would try to put on this face like everything was okay, (might say this is a recurring theme in my life.) I would try to pretend that I was okay with everything happening because "I know God has it all, so I guess I am happy!"

One day, I was lying in bed and was in a pretty rough spot. As I was laying in bed, I heard the Lord say, "Do you know I am not afraid of your anger?" At that moment, I began to just unload everything I had been feeling. My anger about having to be so far from my family. My sadness that school was not going the way I expected it to. My frustration of not understanding what I was supposed to be doing. I unloaded everything. I fell asleep at some point and when I woke up, I expected to feel ashamed, or like the Lord was mad at me, but I experienced the exact opposite. I felt a comfort I had never known before.

The rest of that year, the Lord continued to show me what it looked like to be in full relationship with Him. After all, we are called into a full relationship, which means full emotions. I realized God wanted not just the highs and lows, but everything in between. The moment I let the Lord in on all of my emotions was the moment that I felt an intimacy with Him I never even imagined possible.

Emotions and the church

One of my biggest struggles in life is believing that other people care about my emotions. So often in life, we go through things alone because we hold on to this idea that people don't care or that we are not important enough to share our emotions. As Christians, we always say that we want to be there for people and love people unconditionally, and if this is our standpoint, then my question is, why do so many people in the church feel uncomfortable with talking about their emotions?

If we as a church want to be there for people in their darkest moments, then we need to show them it is not only their worst and best parts of life we care about, but that we care about their lives as a whole. It is far too common in churches for people to go through things and not tell anyone about it because they either believe that their problems are not important enough or that people do not care about what they are going through. The real question is, if so many churches yearn for authenticity and community, then where is the disconnect with people feeling as though they can bring their problems to other people?

If we want authenticity, something in our culture needs to shift. I believe this is an entire church culture that needs to shift, because it's not just one or two people struggling with this. I would argue that it is a strong majority of Christians that feel this way. I believe there are many reasons for this, but one of them is that we have glorified being able to be the "strong one."

I fall into this so hard. In my head, it is a part of who I am that I can take a lot of things and not be bothered. Which I would still say is a part of who I am. The problem is when I am bothered, I still keep it to myself because in the deepest part of me, I hate feeling weak. I believe at times we glorify this idea of "strength", but having weakness doesn't make you any less strong. Recognizing your weakness strengthens you.

I believe another reason we see so many people struggle to bring their problems to others in the church or even their pastor is because we put such a high emphasis on happiness and trust. I think there is a deep-rooted lie in so many of us that says if I am not happy, then I am not trusting what God has for me. The last thing we want to do is admit to ourselves, God, or anyone else that we may be in that spot. What I realized a few years ago was that hiding my sadness, anger and fears from the Lord was only keeping me from experiencing Him.

If you read the Psalms, you see David go through every emotion. And in those prayers and songs, I see such an intimacy with God. After all, David was a man after God's own heart. I believe that part of that reason was because all of David's heart was Gods. Not just the cheerful side, but the doubt, the anxiety, the sadness, everything. If we want our culture to truly resemble Christ, we need to operate under the belief that our emotions not only matter, but are important to God and the people around us.

If we want people to bring their problems, we need to be prepared to not only listen, but to partner with them to help them through it. So often in small groups or discussions with friends, the only thing that ends up being said is "Just remember, Gods got it!" Which is of course true, but not the most helpful thing you can say. In all honesty I think that phrase has become a bit of a cop out for people to not actually have to help each other through things. Communities are meant to walk through things with each other, not just give verbal affirmation. I know for me personally, I know God's got it. What I need is to know that people are prepared and willing to walk alongside whatever is going on in my life.

One of my favorite things about my dad is the way he responds when one of his kids goes through a hard time. He never tells us we will get through it or that it will be okay. He always says to hang in there. It wasn't until I had graduated college that I realized how important that was. Because the truth is, you might fail a class, you might lose a job, things might not get better. It's about persevering through those moments. One reason that my dad saying "hang in there" is so important to me is because I know without a doubt in my mind, he is hanging in there with me. That is what I believe the church should look like. Of course, reassure people that God has it, but at the end of the day, make sure the people in your life know that you are right there with them.

How does the media impact our emotions?

Television shows and movies do an amazing job of manipulating the viewers' emotions in order to make them feel exactly what they want them to feel. They can make totally revolting ideas sound like amazing ones. Don't believe me? Here are some examples:

In the Netflix show *You,* Joe is portrayed as a remarkably charismatic guy who has a tendency to kill people when he falls in love. In the second season, his first girlfriend (who he tried to kill) comes back and is trying to ruin his life. They portray her as the antagonist, and throughout the second season I noticed that rather than rooting for her, I was rooting for Joe, the person I knew was a serial killer. I hated her because the producers did such a skillful job at making Joe, the protagonist, look like a hero that they made you forget in the moment that he is actually the bad guy.

That TV show and many others tell stories in ways that can change the way we see things, even if it is just momentary. Watching shows like this in developmental years can cause a part of our brain to tell us that when we get into relationships, it is okay if they have toxic or unhealthy traits. In that show it only affects us for a moment before we come to our senses and realize that he is the bad guy, but if one show can change the way we feel about a serial killer, then watching shows that continuously have the same stereotypes and stigmas in them can affect how we behave. If you aren't convinced by that one, try this one.

You are at a wedding of one of your dear friends. It is beautiful, everything is amazing. One of his closest friends, who also is his ex, ends up being able to make it at the last minute. Everything is perfect, that is until the groom says the name of his ex instead of the bride.

Now let's assume for some weird reason the bride continues on with the wedding. To make matters worse, when she arrives at the airport after deciding to give him another chance, she sees him boarding the plane with the same girl whose name he said at the altar. When she is talking to you about it a few weeks later, she asks if you think it is reasonable to ask her now husband to no longer see the girl whose name he said instead of hers.

If you're like me, I would say absolutely. I think it is a surprisingly reasonable request, and I think most people would agree. For most people, I would say it is a toned down response for saying the wrong name at the altar. For some reason, in the hit show Friends (my favorite show of all times) when Emily is put in that position, fans look at her as a neurotic crazy woman who is asking too much of her husband. However, if that happened in any of my friends' lives, I would consider them to be extremely reasonable.

The point is the things we are watching can affect our mindsets. I experienced this first hand a few months into being on TikTok. I had been single for over six years and was very happy with that life. I knew I wanted to get married, but I was also very happy with how my time being single had played out and was content with being single as long as I felt the Lord on it. I was even a few months into writing this book, so I thought I had a pretty good grasp on how to not let the media manipulate my emotions.

About four months after getting TikTok, I was fairly deep into single TikTok. I wasn't on thirst traps or anything. Mostly, what I would see was a brief clip of a cute couple followed by someone single reacting in a funny way. I had just moved to New York for an internship and I realized about a month in that I was craving a relationship like I never had before. Suddenly, all I could think about was what life would be like when I was married or wonder why I wasn't in a relationship. My thoughts spiraled pretty quickly and for about two weeks I was so confused as to why I was suddenly so discontent with being single. Was it spiritual warfare? Was it the Lord releasing me to start dating? (that's what I was hoping to be honest.) Was it living in a new place where I hadn't found community yet? I had no idea.

One day I felt the Lord prompting me to look into it deeper and felt a powerful push to look a little closer at my social media. I realized that for a pretty decent amount of time, the content I was putting into my brain was purely of people wanting to be in a relationship. I immediately changed what was coming up on my For You page and within two days, I was back to feeling secure in my singleness. What I had been working on with God for six years was threatened by a few weeks of social media. What you are putting in your mind matters.

In the next few chapters, I will break down some things I learned when looking back at how the media has affected my life. As I go through it, I want you to keep in mind these things we just talked about. Don't just take my word for it, ask yourself in all the things I will go through how this has looked in your life.

Casting
the
Characters

Chapter Four:

The Drama Triangle

One area of relationships that I think gets overlooked is how the media is affecting our friendships. Television shows have some strength in this area on the surface, but when you look deeper into the relationships, you can see that they are actually very unhealthy. You constantly see friends stabbing each other in the back, leaving each other in the dust, getting revenge on each other, not truly listening, and so much more. It shows constant drama. I believe that this has caused us to raise up a generation that believes drama is needed in their relationships. A generation that sees a relationship without drama as boring and not real. I have heard it many times when talking about drama. "Well, it's just a part of life" and is just something we have to deal with... Is it though? Or is it something we have convinced ourselves we have to deal with?

One reason I believe *The Office* and *Friends* are so popular is, yes, because of the amazing comedy, but also because of the friendships that are portrayed in the shows. These relationships are things we strive for. Relationships we dream about and hope to have someday in our lives. I worry, though, that sometimes we get too caught up dreaming about what this could look like and miss it in our own lives. I have heard people say that *Friends* supported them more than their actual friends in hard times, but do we actually give people the chance to support us?

We get so busy watching these shows and thinking it's something that is unattainable, when the truth is it is very attainable. It is just more inconvenient than sitting in bed and watching a show. One of my favorite things about both these shows is the strength of the relationships within them. To watch and know that anything can happen and they will still be there for each other. It is easy to look at life and think, "Wow, why don't I have a community like that?" When the real question is, am I giving people the opportunity to love me in that way? And a better question: am I loving people like that? I can sit there and wish all day for a community like that, but it comes down to if I give people the opportunity to have a genuine part in my life.

Before we get deeper into what shows tell us about friendships, I want to give you a summary of this idea called The Drama Triangle. I think this is important because this idea of a drama triangle is shown in most teen dramas, and I believe it has leaked into a lot of our lives and friendships.

The Drama Triangle

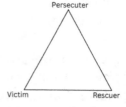

In college, I learned about a theory called Karpman's Drama Triangle. It looks like this. Karpman uses these three roles to describe conflict.

The **Victim**: Is in need of someone else to come to their rescue to make them feel happy or safe.

The **Rescuer**: You take control of someone else's life in order to feel powerful.

The **Persecutor**: Uses control and manipulation to protect yourself or those around you.

One of my favorite moments from my classes in college was the moment my professor finished explaining the drama triangle and began explaining how to get out of it. In his words, the way to exit the drama triangle is by being a "grown-ass person," by stopping the blame game and recognizing the part that you play in every situation. Understanding that even if something happens to you, you have the power to react to it. You can choose to continue to be the victim or the rescuer or the persecutor, or you can see that you are bigger than that. It is your choice to leave it. It is up to you to stop falling into the routine and conflict of the triangle. Instead of waiting for someone to rescue, the actual solution is to have a conversation. To pull up a chair and listen to what the other person has to say, but the norm is to view conflict as a boxing match where usually everyone ends up losing.

We have lost value in relationships and put value in being right ahead of our relationships. I would say that most conflicts I have seen, on any scale, could have been solved if people had been willing to put away the gloves and pull up a chair. Being right should never be as important as the relationship. In any relationship, you will find disagreements, and the only way to keep your relationships is to be okay with disagreeing with a person because the relationship is worth more than you being right.

Most media presence shows us the opposite. Our world has bought into the narrative stating if someone has a fundamental disagreement, there is no way to get along. We separate our relationships into heroes and villains, and it is a lot easier to become someone's villain than it is their hero.

While these roles may switch around in different relationships you are in, many people find their one role that helps them feel powerful. I have seen this triangle play out many times in my own life, but never as drastically as it was in one particular relationship. I had a young woman, let's call her Denise, whom I mentored for years. Throughout these years, without realizing it, we were constantly flowing in and out of this triangle. Denise was constantly the victim of something. While I was constantly rescuing her from whatever or whoever the newest persecutor was. I was always there to rescue her. It came to where, while I was in college, I would repeatedly go to her house to pick her up multiple times a week in order to talk through what happened and try to help in whatever way I could. This happened for years, and it was draining.

Then one day, the roles switched. I became the persecutor while Denise remained the victim. I remember getting a text from her about something that she heard I had said and her getting very upset over something that had not happened in the way she thought it had. This was not too long after I had taken the class that went through this drama triangle, and I recognized the only way I could get out of this toxic triangle: to be a grown-ass person. (Christian author Danny Silk calls it being a powerful person. I just prefer my college professor's version.) I decided at that moment that I would not play in the triangle anymore. Instead of trying to defend myself or try to switch to being the rescuer, I decided to just apologize.

I apologized and told her it did not happen the way she thought, but that I was sorry if she took it the wrong way. She responded again in hatred and anger, to which I replied that I had apologized, and that's all I could do. I told her that she could accept my apology, or she could continue to be angry and not talk to me. She chose the latter, and we did not talk for six months.

This was one of the hardest things I have had to do. I had mentored this girl for years, walked her through her first relationship, through her life's problems, through fights, through everything, and I loved her with everything inside of me. Ending the triangle is difficult, but it's worth it. Six months after that fight, she reached out to me to apologize and accept responsibility for the way she had treated me. We rekindled our friendship, but things were not the same after that point. Not in a bad way, but in a way that relationships change and in that moment I knew that in order to have a healthy relationship with her, I needed to have more boundaries.

Here's the thing. If you are stuck in the triangle, you have to become a powerful person in order to end the cycle in your own life. If you are going to end it, you need to do it with a heart of "this is best for me" not "I am tired of the other person and want them to feel pain." In order to end this drama triangle, you have to end with a heart of love and forgiveness towards the people who are also involved. It would have been very easy for me to have ended up in the victim's corner while trying to leave the triangle. The key is to recognize that it is not about who is the victim or who is the villain, it's about ending the cycle.

We were made to live life in relationships with other people. Unfortunately, a lot of the influence we have right now for relationships is showing unhealthy tendencies. If we want to have a life of healthy relationships, then we have to become powerful, grown-ass people who step out of the triangle and into what relationships should look like.

If you think about it, this is the plot for almost any movie or show you watch. There is a victim who is wronged by a villain. The villain is then stopped by the hero who saves the victim. This plot sequence has entered our lives to where conflict is played out this way rather than being handled in a way that benefits everyone.

In most television shows I have watched, there is drama in every single relationship. A show without drama would be very boring, but when we watch those shows most of our free time, it leaks into our lives. I believe that this has caused us to raise up a generation that believes drama is needed in their relationships. This is a subconscious thing that happens. Obviously most of us don't see a situation and think, "What would Chandler Bing do?" But just because we do not think that way does not mean that those characters have not affected us in some small ways.

You are what you eat. So, when the main thing you are taking in is drama... there is a good chance you are putting out that same drama. I am not saying not to watch these shows; I am saying that we need to:

1. Be aware of the impact they can have.

2. Cut back on the time we are spending with make-believe people

3. Increase the time we spend in genuine relationships

4. I want you to keep this triangle in mind as we dive deeper into the rest of this chapter and see how you think it plays into each of these ideas.

Gossip

"And he called the people to him and said to them, "Hear and understand: it is not what goes into the mouth that defiles a person, but what comes out of the mouth; this defiles a person."Then the disciples came and said to him, "Do you know that the Pharisees were offended when they heard this saying?"He answered, "Every plant that my heavenly Father has not planted will be rooted up. Let them alone; they are blind guides. And if the blind lead the blind, both will fall into a pit."But Peter said to him, "Explain the parable to us."And he said, "Are you also still without understanding? Do you not see that whatever goes into the mouth passes into the stomach and is expelled? But what comes out of the mouth proceeds from the heart, and this defiles a person. For out of the heart come evil thoughts, murder, adultery, sexual immorality, theft, false witness, slander. These are what defile a person. But to eat with unwashed hands does not defile anyone." Matthew 15:10-20 (ESV).

Gossip is one of the most justified sins. Scripture clearly states that what comes out of our mouths defiles us, but we still use every excuse imaginable to excuse our gossip. We have not only accepted gossip as something that has to be in our lives, but we have made it one of the overruling powers of conversations.

I have seen so many good relationships end because of gossip. I think it is sad that we end relationships so quickly, but I think it is more sad that we have become so content and even comfortable talking negatively about people. We use every excuse under the sun to defend our bad habit. We say we are just processing or venting, but there is a fine line between processing and gossip.

When I was in college, I spent three years interning with a youth group. One year in particular, we had an excessive amount of drama break out between a group of girls. All of which started because one person heard a rumor that the other was spreading rumors about her. When I was processing with the Lord how to best handle the situation, He began showing me the line between gossip and processing a situation.

I discovered the line of talking about a person and talking about a problem. Talking about the problem focuses on how you feel, not what the other person did. Continuously talking about the person and not the problems is what I think keeps many people in the victim's mindset. Talking about the problem is me focused, talking about the person is focused on them.

Sometimes people seem so much worse than they are because we spend so much time bashing their character to other people that it's hard to tell what is from their actual character and what is from how often we speak ill of them. This is still something that I struggle with. I honestly believe that gossiping is one of the hardest habits to break. I would say this battle is a daily one for me. One that is hard to implement because the majority of us think gossiping is okay, but the truth is that whether the person hears what you say about them or not, life and death are in the power of the tongue. We have become very comfortable speaking death.

"Death and life are in the power of the tongue, and those who love it will eat its fruits." Proverbs 18:21 (ESV)

The things that come out of our mouth matters. We have come so far in our generation from this idea. We believe that

51

gossip is okay as long as it is just to our best friend, or to our significant other, but the truth is gossip is gossip no matter how you want to sugarcoat it, and gossip is harmful to every person involved.

PLEASE do not hear me wrong. I think it is very important to talk through things going on in our lives, but there is a difference in saying "This happened at work today and I am trying to process it" and "my boss is a horrible person." I believe in processing things going on in our lives, but too often we use "processing" as an excuse to gossip. One key way to tell if you are gossiping or processing, is the amount of people you go to. If you have to go to fifteen different people to "process" something then you are no longer processing. You are gossiping.

Prayer Request Gossip

In the previous chapter, we talked about reasons that people do not tend to open up in church. I believe a big reason is what I will call prayer request gossip. This is where someone goes to a person and asks for prayer, and then that person passes it to their whole small group, and all of the sudden the entire church knows. This concept has to change. We cannot continue to break the trust of people by spreading their prayer requests. If you are trusted with a prayer request, keep it between you and God. If it is something you feel like more people should be praying on, simply ask that person if they are okay with you sharing it with the rest of the prayer team.

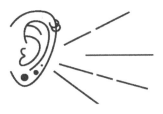

Chapter Five:

I'll Be There For You

In everything we watch, we are presented with a narrative. Something that tells us what is right, what is wrong and what is in the gray area. Every show we watch presents us with a different narrative, but there are common ideals that are spread throughout the cinematic world. There are patterns to the way they show friendships, romantic relationships, parents, and even sex. The trick is learning how to decode what we are being shown and compare that to how healthy and biblical relationships look. This chapter is dedicated to presenting some common things we see represented in friendships, how those themes could be leaking into our lives, and how to recognize what relationships should look like.

The burden of feeling like a burden

The thing I have heard more than anything during my time in ministry is, "I just don't want to be a burden." I've heard that in every situation, from heartbreak to the loss of a family member, to dealing with addiction. I have said it to myself just as many times as I have heard it said by others. The question is, where did we get this idea that sharing what we are going through makes us a burden?

Everyone's answer to where they got that mindset is probably different. Some may have believed it came from a family member, a friend, a teacher, or so many other people. What constantly shocks me is how many people feel as though sharing their pain and struggles makes them a burden. Which made me ask the question: How do we change our culture to stop seeing people's problems as a burden and start seeing them as people who need us?

I saw a post from one of my friends on Facebook a while back that said something like "I would rather listen to your story than listen to your eulogy." which is great and I agree with it completely. However, something about it rubbed me the wrong way. This is nothing against the person who posted it. I love them very much and believe in their heart, but the truth is most people who have contemplated suicide have tried to reach out, and

People will rarely come flat out and say that they are thinking about ending their life and need someone to listen. Because getting to that point is a series of times adding up where they had reached out but got rejected because people did not see it as life or death. We, as a culture, need to learn how to listen when it is not a matter of life or death.

Getting rid of the burden mentality

In order to believe truths, we have to uproot the lie that caused our belief to be misguided. For each person, this may look a little different, but there are things we can each do in order to help us figure out where the lie is rooted. This is what the process looks like for me.

First, I start with worship. For me, that looks like putting on my Spotify playlist. It just needs to be whatever you do to feel closest to the Lord. From there, I trace the lie back. I have had this take anywhere between a few hours, to a few months. There is no correct timeline, especially if it is a deep-rooted lie. The best time to trace it back is after I have had an experience where the lie I am believing comes up.

Doing this requires you to be extremely real with yourself and look back on your past and see where this lie got started and how it has been strengthened over the years. Once you have recognized the lie, break partnership with it. Enter into prayer and ask the Lord to break the mindset you have that feeds into the lie you are believing. From there, I set up a system in my mind to walk myself through anytime that it resurfaces.

For example: When I was struggling with anxiety, I had this lie that I partnered with that said that people either don't remember me after brief interactions or that people don't want to be around me. In social situations, this would look like me not going up to people because I felt like I would not be wanted. After a lot of processing and going back through my past, I could recognize that it was from times in middle and high school where a group of people would not let me hang out with them.

That was the initial planting of the lie. From there, I broke partnership with it. There are still plenty of days where that old habit comes up, and so I talk myself through it. I remind myself that I am loved by many people and that people enjoy being around me. I remind myself that I am not a burden to people, but that there is a fairly good chance they would appreciate me coming up to them and letting them know I remember them and want to be around them. I have even changed my mindset to think that I would rather someone think I am weird because they do not remember me, then hurt someone's feelings because I did not say hi to them. Some days I have to talk myself through it more than others, but it's important to remember to have grace towards yourself.

I still sometimes struggle with this idea that I am being a burden to someone, but I have also seen incredible fruit when I stop thinking that I am burdening people. It has led me to feel more loved by people and opened doors for me to love people in a much more real way.

How to create a culture of not feeling like a burden

In order to create an atmosphere where people feel safe and wanted, we have to figure out ways in which we are making others feel like a burden. This one is tough for me, because in my heart I know I love people and want them to feel safe, but I also am coming to recognize that there are moments where I do not excel at showing love. I have been in conversations where in my mind I am just wondering how much longer they will be talking so I can do something else.

Hear me out. There are people who will try to unload everything that ever happens to them without ever giving you a second to speak, which is why we have to learn to set healthy boundaries. However, there are also plenty of experiences people have where they are just in need of someone listening, but end up getting pushed away instead. I think the most important way to transform this thought process is to learn how to actively listen to people.

Active listening

I think most problems could be solved in television dramas if people would just listen to each other. Truly listen. Where the media is at right now, it encourages speaking before you are fully informed or to speak louder rather than listen to what anyone else says. We as a world need to learn how to actively listen.

Active listening means to listen to understand, not listen to respond. What I have learned from life in ministry, is that rarely do people want to hear my opinion on things. Most people just want to feel heard. I know for myself, the second someone comes in and thinks they understand my problem before I have even finished telling them about it, I no longer want to be a part of that conversation. This usually causes me to stop talking to people in general about what is going on in my life. We have to learn how to be a person who listens because we care about what the other person is saying, not a person who listens to have the "perfect" response.

When I was twenty-two, I moved to California to attend ministry school. I remember during that time learning a lot about what healthy relationships look like and realized that a lot of mine were unhealthy. I realized that in most of my relationships, the other person talked all about their life, and I would ask questions and listen actively and give advice or comfort when I felt it needed it, but most of the time that was not reciprocated.

After my first semester of ministry school, I went home for Christmas and I had a ton of coffee dates set up with friends and students to catch up. With everything I learned, I paid more attention to the dynamic, and I saw quickly that even though I had left for four months, very few people asked me about my time in California or what I had learned or anything that happened. Even when I would bring it up, the topic would quickly switch back to them.

Don't get me wrong, the blame is more on myself than anything because I let my relationships develop that way. I believe there are relationships where that is an okay dynamic, such as the students I mentor, but what I discovered is that my students were more invested and asked me more questions when I met with them than my friends did. It was at that moment that I had to make a very hard decision to limit the amount of people I hang out with. (I am an enormous people pleaser so this was very hard.)

I kept relationship dynamics to where it was healthy for me too, which involved a lot of seeing who would reach out when I came back into town and who would let the dynamic switch to a mutual dynamic. When I did this, I noticed I was significantly happier and when the relationships became equal; the dynamics became so much deeper. Once I made the switch, I had much stronger relationships, and I felt significantly less drained.

TV teaches us to be quick to talk. The people who talk first are the leaders or the important people, but it is so important to be slow to speak and quick to listen. We need to learn that our opinion is not always the most important thing that needs to be heard. I have seen so many relationships struggle because one person thought their voice was more important than the others. If you want strong relationships with emotional depth, you have to be willing to listen and to leave the drama triangle and enter an equally balanced relationship.

If we want to change the narrative that says people are burdens, then we have to reprogram our minds to not see people that way. We have to listen to people when they have something going on instead of being annoyed and wishing we were doing other things. If we want our problems to matter to others, then other people's problems need to matter to us. To stop this toxic idea of people feeling like burdens, we have to be the first to step up and recognize how we can change that.

People don't change

This is one area where I think shows do an excellent job, but we do not follow the example. In every teen drama that I have ever watched, there is a character who seems unredeemable, who ends up being loved and a much better person at the end. In my opinion, it's how you can tell how good a show is. It's character development. People like Klaus Mikelson, Damon Salvatore, Rumplestiltskin, and even Chuck Bass go from being the worst of the worst to someone we end up loving.

Yet for some reason, this idea has not crossed over into our world. We tend to believe that people just do not change. As Christians, we should be the people most against this idea. The entire gospel is a story of redemption, yet so often we hold this idea that people just don't change. We are especially bad about this when we know the person who is changing. We are amazing at hearing testimonies of people leaving lives of addictions, gossip, heartache, etc, and celebrating those. Where we struggle is when someone we know changes.

This is one I have struggled with when I see someone who I maybe did not have a high fondness of becoming a better person. My first thought is usually "It's not real" instead of choosing to celebrate with them that God is changing their life. We have to change this culture of saying people don't change, or immediately canceling people because we disagree with them. We have to give people the opportunity to change. I firmly believe that one of the most prominent reasons we don't see people change is because we do not give them the room in which to change. It's called a self-fulfilling prophecy. Basically, what that means is that if you continuously tell someone they are going to fail, they will eventually believe it themselves and stop trying. If we do not believe that people can change, then we do not believe in the full transformative power of God.

We see this concept constantly in scripture, but most notably is Paul. Paul was a murderer, and was transformed by the power of God and affected the church in massive ways, including writing a good majority of the New Testament. If we can believe in a mass murderer's transformation, why can't we believe in the transformation of someone at work?

Communication

In every relationship, be it romantic or otherwise, communication is a huge component of how healthy and life giving those relationships are. Shows and movies very rarely have healthy communication, if they have any communication at all. A lot of times we see people rely on arguments that end in people going their own way and doing whatever they think is best rather than communicating with each other to get on the same page. We also see people solely relying on sarcasm in order to avoid communication (something I am very guilty of.)

In any book you read on healthy relationships, they say that communication is the most important aspect, and yet we ignore that all the time. So often we think "well if they just understood how I felt then this would be over." Have you ever stopped to think that they are thinking the same thing? That maybe there are two sides to every story, but we get so wrapped up in our own side we forget to ask about the other. Communication helps us to see things how they are meant to be seen.

The Big Bang Theory

I honestly believe that most sitcoms actually do a fairly good job of showing how a lack of communication can affect a situation. I chose The Big Bang Theory because half of the premise of this show is people who think differently trying to do life together. You have Penny, who is of average intelligence, Leonard, Howard, Bernadette and Raj, who are above average intelligence and Sheldon and Amy, who are geniuses. They each have their own social quirks, which leads to a hilarious show of them trying to live life together.

I think this show is good to look at when concerning communication because they each have to learn in their own way how to communicate effectively with others in the group. You can see through Sheldon's journey that a lot of the issues he has are because he doesn't really understand how a normal person's brain works, which causes him to hurt people or do something weird without realizing it. As the show goes on, you can see each character learning to lean more into healthy ways of communication so that they are able to have a powerful community.

One of my favorite episodes of the show is Season 7 Episode 1. In this episode, Penny is trying to get Sheldon to tell her something personal. After some probing, he mentions YouTube changed something on their interface that has been bothering him. She gets up frustrated to leave, at which point Sheldon says, "Here's something else you don't know about me. You just hurt my feelings." Penny responds with "I didn't think it was a big deal" to which Sheldon responds "It is to me, that's the point." Penny apologizes and they end up having a nice heart to heart moment.

We get so transfixed in our lives thinking that the people around us are bothered by the same things. Often in life, we end up doing exactly what Penny did. We take something that is really important to another person and pretend that it is nothing. Most of the time, we do not even realize that we hurt the other person's feelings. I love this episode of The Big Bang Theory because for most of the show you watch under the impression that Sheldon is always hurting everyone else's feelings but in this episode they flip the narrative to show you that there were probably a lot of times his feelings were hurt as well. In order to have healthy communication and relationships, we have to realize that not everyone finds the same things as important as we do.

Sitcoms and community

Sitcoms are one of my favorite things to watch. Shows like Friends, The Office, The Big Bang Theory, New Girl, and Parks and Rec. I love them all. These shows are the shows I go to for comfort, to laugh, to bond with friends and so much more. I know they have played a similar role in a lot of other people's lives. The comedy is of course amazing, but I think there is another reason that we have such a love for these types of shows.

One day while I was sitting with the Lord, I wondered why we love shows like that so much. One reason is definitely the wit, but I think it goes deeper than that. I believe we find those types of shows so intriguing because we want that life for ourselves. A life where you have a solid group of friends who love you deeply and fiercely through anything and everything and who are there for the big moments just as much as they are for the small moments.

One important thing you see in those shows is their authenticity with each other, as well as their willingness to talk about their crap. As I mentioned in Chapter 3, it is up to us to bring our emotions to the table and by doing that, we can create the community we see in these shows. Think about it. In all of those shows, every character knows everything about each other. When Ross got divorced each time, he went to his friends. When Monica lost her job, she went to the rest of them for comfort. When Marshall's dad died in How I Met Your Mother, he immediately went to his friends. The list goes on and on; the point is they did not hide from their friends. That is what I believe makes these shows so worth watching.

In order to receive the love we all want so desperately, we have to be open to it. We have to be open to the idea of being fully known by someone else. To be seen through shame, through low self-esteem, through struggles, through it all. We have to change our mindset that says I cannot be loved until I have reached a certain place in life. That we cannot be loved until we are perfect. If we don't change our mindset, then we are chasing a dream that will never come true.

In order to be loved and show unconditional love, we have to recognize the One who loved us first. We have to open up our hearts to say that we are okay with being seen as we are, and not as we want to be or how we think we should be. There is no place we can reach that earns us love. We have to stop reaching for love and start receiving it.

We were made to live in a community. We were made to live life in the presence of other people, to do life with them, feel their embrace, to be encouraged and loved. Now, I see less and less genuine community, so now we are relying on television to fill that void.

I am highly extroverted. If I am not around people, I go crazy. For those who are not familiar with introverts and extroverts, or have some confusion, being an extrovert does not mean being outgoing. Being an extrovert means I get my energy from being around people. Being an introvert means you get your energy from your alone time. It has nothing to do with how outgoing or shy you are; it is purely where you get your energy from. What I have noticed is that the need to be around people is less when I watch TV when I am alone. Why? Because it gives the illusion of being around people. If it can energize an extrovert, then it definitely can give the illusion that you have people in your life. It is like drinking coffee instead of sleeping. It is a temporary fix and is not as effective as if you just went to bed. This is the same way. It may fix your problems for a time, but eventually you need the real thing.

Odds are that the time with your temporary fix can be bad for your mental health. You miss so much of what we were created for. We miss the embraces of people, the laughs of stories, the love you feel with people who know you. Because when you watch TV, you may know them like the back of your hand, but that is a one-way street. There is a reason that every year, anxiety rises, depression rises, suicide rates are rising and not only are they rising, but they are setting in at younger ages. It's because we are lonely, but have a distraction from loneliness. A distraction that allows us not to deal with the genuine problems in our lives. We no longer search for community. Before television, if you didn't spend time with people, you sat in your room staring at a wall, but now we have the option to constantly be engulfed in other people's stories. We need the true company of other people. We need more than meaningless conversations, more than what we receive at school or work in brief interactions. We need real people who know us and who we know.

Even Jesus did life with others, and if Jesus needed community, then so do we. The community of Jesus looks very different from the community we think of. The Biblical community looks like eating together, doing ministry together, as well as calling people higher, rebuking when needed, and loving above all.

I believe that one problem we have in the community is that we sometimes forget how to critique lovingly. We are taught from shows that being right is more important than relationships, and that when someone disagrees with you, it's okay to walk away from the relationship.

Working through conflict helps relationships grow deeper, so when we leave any relationship after a little conflict, that leaves us with very shallow relationships. We need to learn how to lovingly call people higher, as well as how to lovingly accept differences. When we work through conflict, we are left with deeper connection, but when you live in a passive aggressive world, it makes it hard to go that deep. The shows we watch say that people should just know what they did wrong, it's always on the other person to make the first step to apologize or both parties will just forget and will lovingly embrace while crying and saying I forgive you but that is not real life. If both people have the mindset of waiting for the other to apologize, there will never be reconciliation.

In real life, there is a lot of time people do not even realize they have done something wrong, or they are waiting for you to make the move. Connection comes when you are willing to say I care about my relationship with you more than I care about being right at this moment.

The right to be right

We are in a culture where we value being right over the relationship. It is more important to us to win a fight on Facebook, or argue with someone to make sure they recognize they are wrong, instead of valuing a relationship more than whatever the argument is.

I am a queen at winning dumb arguments about random things, such as if a hamburger is a type of sandwich (it is). However, the second I am in a discussion where I see there is a potential to ruin a relationship, I decide to die to my pride because I care more about the person than whatever argument we are having. If there is a discussion about a political candidate that I disagree with, the second it gets hostile, I choose not to push it. Not because I do not have firm beliefs, I do, but it is not worth it to ruin a relationship. That does not mean that I do not let my opinions out or stand up for what I believe in, but once I have made my point, I see no point to argue further, especially if the other person is arguing just to be mad about something.

I live for lively discussions, and discussions about hard topics. I think it is a very important thing in life to know where you stand in life on certain subjects. Just not as important as showing love to another person. Anytime I watch a show, I see very little of this portrayed. It is usually a "my way or the highway." I am not saying denounce what you believe to keep a relationship, I am saying stop the argument. You do not even have to tell them they are right, just a simple "I see what you are saying and I respect your opinion."

As Christians, we need to remember that our duty is to love, and sometimes that means seeing through another lens. We can see this represented biblically in 1 Corinthians 8:12-13. Paul states, "Thus, sinning against your brothers and wounding their conscience when it is weak, you sin against Christ. Therefore, if food makes my brother stumble, I will never eat meat, lest I make my brother stumble."

The entire chapter is really a great example of what it looks like to love rather than argue. Paul shows here that even though he knows the Lord said it is okay to eat meat, if he is around someone who views it as sin he will not eat to keep his relationship with them, rather than eating meat with them because he does not see it as a sin.

There are extremes to this, you should never go into sin because someone else views it as okay. The point Paul is making is to remember it's about love, it is not about being right. In that same chapter, Paul tells us that knowledge puffs up, while love builds up.

We pray for God to make Himself known to us and the world, but then seconds later, open up the social media apps on our phone. Do you want to know how God makes it pretty clear that His presence will be shown to the world? It's through His people. It's through us. If the world isn't seeing the amount of Jesus we want, then maybe we should look at just how much we are doing to show the world Jesus.

Nathan Teeters once said, "The world would be a different place if the church started to redeem the times instead of begging to be rescued from them." If we want to see Jesus redeem the times, He called us to be His vessels, so maybe we should take that a little more seriously. We can post as many times as we want that picture on Facebook that says Jesus loves, but until we live that out, we will continue to see the world in chaos.

John 13:35 (ESV) *says, "By this, all people will know you are my disciples, if you have love for one another."*

I would say right now Christians are more known for hating and criticizing people in their own religion than they are known for love.

If you want the world to know Jesus, if you want the world to look different, we have to take Jesus' commands to love God and love people more seriously. Love is more than posting something on Facebook. It's a lifestyle. It's extending grace to the person who cut you off. It's taking a few minutes out of your day to hear about someone else's. The world has the stigma on Christians that says we are judgmental and rude. Instead of saying that it's not true, show them what love truly looks like.

If someone has had an unpleasant experience with Christians, it is not my job to redeem the church; it is my job to show them the love of Christ. I refuse to sit somewhere and try to convince someone that they just had an unpleasant experience and that not everyone is that way. I want my actions to redeem the experience they had. Trying to convince someone that their experience is not typical of all Christians may not work, but showing them what it looks like to actively live a Christ-filled life can.

We have grown into a society that has to be right. You have to see my point and agree with me, otherwise you are not loving me. If we want to show the world the love of Jesus, we have to give up our right to be right, and step into our call to love. If being right costs you your relationship, it's not worth it. I am not saying to compromise your belief system; I am saying set your pride down. In conversations, if you can tell it's getting too heated, instead of continuing, say "listen, I know we disagree, and that's okay, but I want you to know I care way more about you than I care about this disagreement."

Again, we can all say this easily, but living it is a different story. For example, if you care more about making sure someone knows being a democrat or republican is wrong more than you care about making them know the Lord loves them, you need to re-prioritize. God does not need us to defend His honor. I promise you; He is capable of that. What He commanded us was to love. We are called above EVERYTHING to love. Media tells us love is contingent, Jesus proved love is unconditional. That none of us deserve it, but He willingly gave His life so that I could live mine. Because of that, I choose to love with the same love that was given to me. In the same way that Jesus looked past the prostitute and saw a daughter, past the corrupt tax collector to see a son, past Peter's betrayal to see his loyalty, we need to choose to look past disagreement, and see a child of the King.

That brings us into what we are going to talk about for the next bit. I want to talk to y'all about who you are with while you are walking with Christ.

68

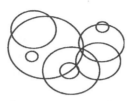

Chapter Six:

The Inner Circles

Relationships and community were given to us to help us navigate life and grow in our relationships with Christ. We need to recognize how relationships are meant and how they are portrayed by us now. I think that there are times when movies, shows and social media do a great job of showing unconditional love of friends, but they also give unrealistic expectations and attributes to friends. In order to combat this we need to know how God intended us to do relationships.

Jesus' Relationships

As a Christian, my goal is to be like Jesus in every aspect of my life, including relationships. Jesus showed us what it looked like to live in community with others. What it looks like calling people higher and handling conflict with love. When Peter goes against what God is asking, Jesus says directly to Peter, "Get behind me Satan." He does not wait to go to the rest of the disciples later to talk about what happened behind Peter's back. He addresses Peter at the moment and keeps the relationship. In an easily offendable world, it feels like the safer option is to not call things out, but as Christians, we are meant to call our friends higher.

One of the most impactful moments of how I viewed relationships was when I realized the significance of Jesus' relationships after the resurrection. A few years ago I was in a small group with the youth group I interned for and the question was asked "what does the resurrection of Jesus mean to you." The day before, I had been watching Game of Thrones. If you are not past season 5 of the show, I suggest skipping this next paragraph. In the show, Jon Snow is considered to be a person of noble character. He is very caring, forgiving, brave and level-headed. In the fifth season finale, he was betrayed and killed by some of his own people. In the next season, he is resurrected. He then chooses to leave the people he had promised his whole life to because he could not stand the idea of living with the same people who betrayed him.

When the question was asked about what the resurrection meant to me, a new bell rang in my head. Jesus's relationships didn't change after the resurrection. He strengthened them. He stood there with people who denied him and took him to be murdered and continued to love them and disciple them. Today we live with the idea that when someone wrongs us, I will love them from afar, but that's just Christian lingo, for I no longer care for that person.

We throw a relationship away because we hear from someone that someone else said something about us, and do not even bother to find out if it's true. We just decide that the relationship is over. Shows and movies tell us that when you are betrayed, leave them. We drop people for way less than murder. If someone says something behind our backs, our first instinct is to say "I do not want that person in my life anymore" but, that is not how Jesus showed us to live.

He not only loved, but hung out with the people who watched him be beaten and murdered, and still said I want my relationship with you. He went to them after he was murdered- after they betrayed him. If that is the model we are to follow, we are doing a terrible job.

Relationships should be deeper and more valuable to us than anything, but we choose to see them as something we can throw away because we can always create new ones. And that causes us to feel lonelier and lonelier. We don't have people who know us to our core because we have watched for years people just throw away a relationship. While on the shows they might come back, they do not show what it actually takes to get through conflict.

One of my favorite interactions in scripture is in John 21:15. In this section of scripture, Jesus asks Peter three times if he loves him. All three times Peter answers yes, and Jesus responds with a command. Jesus asks this three times to symbolize the three times Peter denied Jesus. Rather than guilting and shaming Peter after he denied him THREE times, something that I cannot say I would forgive so easily, Jesus simply asks him three times "do you love me."

Biblical Community

In our lives, we have multiple groups of communities. So I briefly want to explain Jesus's communities. The first group of community that Jesus had was with 3 people, Peter James and John. Then it expanded to the 12 disciples, then to the 72 that followed Jesus and expanded more to the crowds.

The groups that I am really going to focus on with you are your 3 and your 12. The group of 3 is your group of closest people, who you dedicate the most time with. The 12 is the group that you still spend a lot of time with, but not as intentional as the 3. The first and most important thing that you need to know is that when you are walking with Christ, you need people to walk with you. We were not made to do anything alone.

If you are one of those people who thinks you can do it on your own, that is not what we are called to do. We are called to live in community with fellow Christians in order to better ourselves and to learn from each other. Jesus did not need a community; he chose to have one. Jesus could have easily done things on his own, but he chose to have people with him as he did these things.

Picture this. You are going on a trip to climb a mountain. You have everything packed and ready to go, and you get there and you are all alone. Do you want to be climbing that mountain by yourself? What if something went wrong? There is no one to help, and you would be alone the whole time. So it should be the same when you are talking about your walk with Christ.

That being said, you want to make sure you have the right people to help you as you are walking through your life, and that everyone's minds and hearts are focused on the right things. You do not want people who do not care about your journey and are not willing to go through every part with you. If you were climbing a mountain and half of the people going with you did not actually want to go on a hike, you would probably end up having a miserable time. Having like-minded people is essential.

Creating a Christian community takes time and effort. You cannot expect your community to be perfect with no work, and even with work there will never be a perfect one, but if you focus your community's eyes on Christ, then you can work to have a community that glorifies God. You need to prepare together and strengthen your community. You wouldn't go on a trip with nothing, you go having already prepared for certain things. Your communities are there to help you through the highs and the lows, to help you learn and grow together. If you have no one in your community, it makes it harder to reach the summit on your mountains. I want to talk to you about how your community can grow together and resemble the community of Jesus and the disciples. The first few characteristics of the community that I want to focus on today are found in Acts 2:42-47. In these verses, I want to point out to you several characteristics of communities that can be seen in this passage.

Acts 2:42-47: *And they devoted themselves to the apostles' teaching and the fellowship, to the breaking of bread and the prayers. And awe came upon every soul, and many wonders and signs were being done through the apostles. And all who believed were together and had all things in common. And they were selling their possessions and belongings and distributing the proceeds to all, as any had need. And day by day, attending the temple together and breaking bread in their homes, they received their food with glad and generous hearts,*

praising God and having favor with all the people. And the Lord added to their number day by day those who were being saved.

The first characteristic is that communities are meant to learn and teach together. If you will look back at verse 42: *And they devoted themselves to the apostles' teaching and the fellowship, to the breaking of bread and the prayers.* The people in your tightest group need to be the people that you learn with and learn from. These are the people that know you the best, and you know the best. Within your community, you need to have times that are focused purely on learning and devoting yourself to God's word so that you may learn from His word and from what each other has to say.

The second thing you can see in this verse is they pray together. And I believe this is one of the most important roles. Prayer is such a powerful tool that we have and we need to make sure and use it to pray for our communities.

In Luke Chapter 22 verse 31 Jesus is talking to Peter and he says:

"Simon, Simon, behold, Satan demanded to have you, that he might sift you like wheat, but I have prayed for you that your faith may not fail. And when you have turned again, strengthen your brothers." Peter said to him, "Lord, I am ready to go with you both to prison and to death." Jesus said, "I tell you, Peter, the rooster will not crow this day, until you deny three times that you know me."

Jesus knew Peter would deny Him. He knew that his faith would fail, but Jesus prayed that Peter's faith would be strengthened and that he would use it to strengthen himself and his brothers. Our prayers can help people through situations. We need to pray for our communities individually and together so that we can be strengthened together.

Notice, Jesus did not pray that he would avoid the temptation; He prayed that through his faults, Peter would end up stronger and that it would strengthen his brothers. Prayer is such a powerful tool, and can be done anywhere and anytime, but we only use it in crisis situations. We need to get into the habit of praying for those around us and for God to grow and strengthen our communities and the people in them, and to stop saying "I'll pray for you" and never actually getting to it. I have been a part of more and more communities now where the second someone says they need prayer, they pray right then. Let me tell you, those moments are extremely powerful.

Continuing on, *"And awe came upon every soul, and many wonders and signs were being done through the apostles."* We are called to bear witness together. In Acts 1, Jesus is preparing to ascend back into heaven, and in verse 8 he says, "But you will receive power when the Holy Spirit has come upon you and you will be my witnesses." Jesus called His disciples to tell people His story together. We are called to tell not only the things that we learn from the Bible but to bear witness to the amazing things we see God do not only in our lives, but the things that we see God do in our friends' lives.

If you fix your eyes on Christ, you will see him moving through your communities.

44 *"And all who believed were together and had all things in common."* This is focused more on your 72. We are not called to live in community with the Christians we like or are more similar to. We are called to gather with all who believe. We need to gather with the people that believe so that we can

learn more and have fellowship with each other. Too often in American Christianity, denominations are separated by one thing or another. I think if we truly want to see God work in America, we have to set aside our differences and recognize that every denomination has something to bring to the table. When we as Christians can't even get along with other Christians, what makes us think the people around us will be in unity?

Verse 45 says

"And they were selling their possessions and belongings and distributing the proceeds to all, as any had need."

The disciples sold their possessions and gave them to the others throughout the nation in order to serve them. We are called to do the same.

If you think about all the things that we have that you don't use, we have so much extra that we do not need. We can use that to help serve. Our communities need to have the mindset of service for the Lord, not for ourselves, so that we can make an impact in our larger areas of community.

46 And day by day, attending the temple together and breaking bread in their homes, they received their food with glad and generous hearts, 47 praising God and having favor with all the people. And the Lord added to their number day by day those who were being saved.

The next thing communities are used for is to grow together. In this verse it shows how the disciples met together daily, with generous hearts. They met together and praised God and He continued to add to their numbers. Our communities are used as discipling tools. Each day, they ate together and went to the temple with each other. They were continuously in each other's presence and were devoting themselves to God.

A question I have for you is when you are with your community, are you really with them, or are you focused on what is happening on your phone? If you are not present with your community, then you cannot create the relationships needed to resemble Jesus and the disciples. Our cell phones are a tool that we can use for our communities, but it should not be the source of our communities.

The source of your community needs to be the Holy Spirit, and you need to be in each other's presence while growing together, not relying on your phone. You need to be present with the people you are with in order to create an effective community.

The next thing that needs to happen in a community is probably one of the hardest things. In your community, part of your job is to tell them when they have gone astray or are not working for the things of the Lord. In Mark 8, Jesus tells the disciples that he is going to be crucified and Peter argues with what he was saying. In Mark 8:32, Jesus rebukes Peter, saying, *"Get behind me, Satan! For you are not setting your mind on the things of God but on the things of man."* When Peter took his eyes off God's plan, Jesus told him that what he was doing was wrong.

Just like that, we need to hold our community accountable when they walk astray or take their eyes off of the Lord's plan and look at worldly things. Now then, I do not want you to take that and start calling your friends Satan when they mess up. Do not do that. But when your friends walk astray, have a conversation with them and try to help them through the situation that is causing them to take their eyes off of God's plan. You need to hold them accountable, just as you need to be held accountable.

As with everything, there is a balance with this. We are not called to keep the entire human race accountable on our own. We are just called to keep the people in our communities accountable, which also means you have to be held accountable.

One reason I believe we are seeing so many people leave the church and want nothing to do with Christianity is because we expect them to look like Christ before we have actually introduced them to Him. We expect people to follow our own convictions and customs the second they walk into the church instead of focusing on first introducing them to the Father. We try to hold the world more accountable than we do our own friend groups. It is with relationships that we are meant to hold each other to certain standards, but none of those standards matter if you have not introduced the person to Jesus first.

Another important thing to know about communities is that they will not always stay the same. In Acts 1, it talks about how after Jesus had ascended, the other disciples found a man named Matthias to replace Judas. It is important to remember that sometimes people will leave your community, and that is okay. Different people will come in and out of your community as your life goes on, but your goal should be to create a community with them that resembles that of the disciples. For example, when you go from middle to high school, high school to college, or college to the real world, your communities will change. This is not a bad thing and is nothing to hold grudges over, it is just a part of life. Whether it's because you move towns, or churches or people change and start taking their eyes off of Christ, things will happen that will change your community, but the idea behind your community needs to stay the same.

These things are characteristics you want to have within your community. In order to be effective and have a community that resembles Christ, we need a community that resembles the ones he created. Your communities are what you need to help you through your mountains as well as your valleys. The journey that you go on will be for you and your walk with Christ, but that does not mean that you have to go through it alone, and it makes it easier when you're not alone.

Chapter Seven:

I Am Who _____ Says I am?

Relationships, as shown through the media, tell us a few things. One of which is that your significant other is your "other half, " the part you have been missing your whole life. It tells us that because of that, we should wear our heart on our sleeves, and put everything we are into a relationship, whether it be physically or emotionally. Scripture tells us to guard our hearts. I believe it is because of that idea of a perfect relationship we see so many people lose themselves anytime they enter a new relationship.

So many people do not know who they are when a relationship ends because we have been taught that our significant others are our other half. We are taught that they complete what we are missing, so when a relationship ends, it feels as though we lost who we are completely. We end up feeling empty because we try to fill a void with a person when that void is meant to be filled by Christ. We all yearn to be loved fully, to have a love so unconditional it would do anything for us. A love that would love us at any point in our lives and accept us through and through.

We have that love available to us, but so many people miss out on that opportunity. When we try to use someone else's love in replacement of Jesus, they will fall short every time. I believe part of the reason we miss the opportunity to be fully loved by Jesus is because we have a false opinion of what love looks like coming from Him. We assume love from the Father comes from being a good Christian or doing the right things, but there is nothing we could do to earn His love.

In the same way, there is nothing we could do to separate us from His love. I have struggled with this mindset for a long time. I would never say it out loud, but in my mind I always would think that once I hit a certain point or did a certain thing, that would be when God would love me more. Because of that, I always found myself striving. I could not comprehend that Jesus loved me just as much when I lost myself in my high school relationship as He does when He sees me preaching on a stage.

He loves me, because He loves me, because He loves me. There is absolutely nothing I can do to change it. We live our lives thinking we need to strive for love. Failure is not an option. It is about how successful you are which determines what you are worth. We put our worth into these things that are so inconsistent, and when something goes wrong, it feels as though we lost ourselves. Whether it is a relationship, a job, a sport, anything, we have created a culture that values success over everything.

In order to feel the love we all crave so desperately, we have to break the mindset that our achievements determine our worth. As I was writing this book, I got stuck in that dilemma. I kept telling myself that when I wrote the book and got it published, that would be the point where I knew I had accomplished something. Where I knew the Lord would be proud of me. Even if only five people read it, it wouldn't matter. I knew the Lord would be proud of me. It was hard for me to recognize the joy the Lord took in my writing. The joy of the Lord that was not contingent on my being published, but was proud of my obedience. In my head, I thought I had done little to be proud of.

After I finished college and moved across the country to attend ministry school, I was "living in the future". In my head, I had this idea of how different I would feel, and how exciting my life would be XYZ years into the future. I thought I had to accomplish something not only for God to be proud of me, but for the people around me to be proud of me. Two weeks before my 24th birthday, I met with my pastor at the school I was attending. In this meeting, she helped me open my eyes to the fact that I have a habit of being too hard on myself. She told me I needed to listen to this song called Inheritance, in which Graham Cook says a line I constantly play in my head. He says, "There is nothing you can do that would make Him love you more. There is also nothing you can do that would make Him love you less. He loves you, because He loves you, because He loves you, because that is what He is like. "

If you've never heard this, I encourage you to stop right here and listen to it. I listened to this song constantly until it opened my eyes to see how the Father loved me. Not my future me, not what I would do, but that He loved me there in that moment in the same way He always has, which is the same way He always will.

We are taught love comes from success. That we earn love and, in order to be loved, we need to give everything we are. I thought I needed to be at a certain place in order to feel the presence of the Lord. As I changed this mindset, my 24th birthday hit. I was away from most of my friends and family, but in almost every text I got, there was something about them being proud of me. Being proud of what I had accomplished, proud of who I was. I remember being overwhelmed with emotion. I didn't feel like I had accomplished anything. I didn't feel worthy of people being proud of me because I was looking at myself with eyes of striving, not eyes of abiding.

We have been trying to get this unconditional love from people. Striving for a love that we can only receive from Christ.

The One who created us. But there is no need to strive. There is no need to reach a certain point in life, because He loves you as you are right at this moment. There is no need to strive. You are the beloved. It is our job to be loved outrageously. This love is always available to us, but we need to learn to receive it. We need to learn to turn our attention to Him and break our mindset that we need to be a certain thing to be loved. When we think that way, we continuously change the finish line, to make it a point we will always chase after but will never reach.

There are so many ways our world is shaping our identities. I want to take some time to walk through some roles and stereotypes I see as having a powerful influence over how we see ourselves.

Stereo types

Entertainment has a habit of setting stereotypes that, however much we try not to live into, more often than not we find ourselves mirroring the stereotype we feel most represents us. I am not talking about racial or gender stereotypes; I am talking about character stereotypes.

These are some of the common character stereotypes I am talking about.

Main characters: kind of annoying and make terrible decisions. Tend to take on the world's problems as their personal problem.

The sidekick: is always there for everyone when they are needed, but has no one to be there for them.

The funny one: is usually not taken seriously and has a rough home life.

The spoiled one: who messes up a lot but can fix it with their money and is usually painfully unaware of the real world.

The player: Hooks up with or dates many people. Most of the time, it is a male character. Usually has parental issues.

The smart one: Often seen as not conventionally attractive, made fun of often, usually type A, seen as a control freak, has a hard time in romance and is often overlooked by the main character.

There are definitely more, but these are the ones I see most often in shows. Each of these character types has a string of stereotypes that go along with them. I am not going to list them out for you; I am sure you can figure them out on your own based on what you watch. I believe most people have one of these characters they fit into. For myself, for a long time, I would put myself into the sidekick role. Feeling like I do all the things for people and don't have people to do the same for me. During high school and college, I can see moments in my life where I leaned into that more and more and would fall into the tropes I would see within the shows I was watching.

I have seen many posts on TikTok talking about how their personality changes based on whoever is their favorite character at the time. Most of them are joking, but I think the truth is we do that. We change parts of who we are to resemble people we see on screen. If we continuously change parts of ourselves based on what we are watching, we can never truly find who we are.

Mistakes do not disqualify us from being loved.

One theme we see a lot throughout media and our culture is this idea that mistakes will brand you for life. So often in life, we take our mistakes to be a part of who we are. If we fail a class, all of a sudden we are just a failure. If we forget to do something someone asked us, we are a bad friend. If we mess up a project at work, we are bad at our jobs. We take on our mistakes as part of our identity. When in reality, mistakes aren't something that should shape our identity, but a tool we should use to strengthen ourselves.

I was living into the lie that said if I made a mistake, then I was not measuring up. I was not being my best self. One day, during a brief devotional time in class, one of our speakers asked "who told you it was not okay to make a mistake?" I racked my mind for the answer to that question. My parents always pushed us to give it our all in life, but always met mistakes with grace. I could not figure out who told me I could not make mistakes, but I knew it was something deeply embedded in me. Anytime I would make any mistake, I would beat myself up. I had no grace for myself.

We put ridiculously hard standards on ourselves. Basically, everyone I know does this. I know very few people who, when they make a mistake, just brush it off like it's not a big deal. Almost everyone I know struggles with this which leads me to believe it was taught from something we all have access to. I think social media plays as big of a role in this issue as film. In Lauren Diagles song You Say, there is a line that says "You'll have all my failures God, you'll have every victory." I didn't realize it the first time I heard the song, but I would come to realize it is a lot easier for me to give God my victories and beat myself up for my failures.

During preach week at my ministry school, I came to learn just how much more attention I gave to failures than I did to victories. This was amid my journey to learning how to preach and fully stepping into that calling on my life.

For years, I was terrified of public speaking. I thought I was terrible at it. My first year of ministry school, God showed me it was actually a lie implanted in me from a very young age. I came out of agreement with that lie and pursued preaching. When preach week came, it was only my fifth or sixth time preaching. During this week, you preach to about 30 other students. I did my sermon, and honestly, it was pretty good. In the end, I got phenomenal feedback. I even got compared to two of my favorite female preachers. Ninety-eight percent of the feedback was amazing, two percent was constructive criticism. The criticism wasn't even really negative; it was my facilitators telling me what they would have liked to see had I had more time, as we only had ten minutes to preach.

When I left that day, I felt defeated. I felt like complete garbage. The only part of my feedback I could remember was the negatives, and I took them very hard. The next day, I felt an urge to go back and listen to the feedback. I immediately kicked myself because I realized so much of it was so positive. In my head I thought "C'mon Ashlee, you got compared to Havilah Cunnington based on that message and all you can do is focus on the negative aspects???" I was so disappointed in myself. I could not recognize the many victories that happened that day, and the love that God was trying to show me at that moment. All I could focus on was the negative.

About a week later, I met with my pastor and she told me this line that I tell myself constantly when I am struggling to see victories or failures. She told me I needed to hold myself to human standards. I ask myself that question constantly when I am struggling. She then asked me to ask God what He thought of that sermon, and I immediately felt overwhelmed with the love of God. He walked me through how proud he was of that moment. It was there I realized I needed to rewire my brain. To stop focusing so hard on the negative. To teach myself it was okay to make mistakes and start training my brain to focus on the positive as much, if not more so, than the negative.

In the shows I watch, one mistake ruins lives. One mistake has catastrophic consequences. Not to say to not expect consequences when you make a mistake, but when I would make a mistake, I would question who I am. Mistakes no longer just show us how we can improve, now in our minds they show us how we are a failure. We are being taught to pay the most attention to the negative. I believe this comes from every single aspect of the media.

On social media, we are being shown how much better other people's lives are. In the news media, we are almost always given more stories about the negative things going on in the world than we are the positive. Finally, in film, we

I Am Who _____ Says I Am

are shown that mistakes are irredeemable. That by making a mistake, you can put others at risk or become a person seen as irredeemable. It shows that the guy who cheats, even if it is not his character, is a terrible person with no chance at redemption. The woman who makes one wrong decision ruins her life. In some shows, mistakes end up getting people killed. While I don't think most of us have a mindset that says mistakes get people killed, it still gives us the mindset that says mistakes are bad and failure is not an option.

Male and Female roles

Male roles

From the time we were young, all we have wanted is that perfect movie type relationship. The perfect love story. Maybe even the breakup that ultimately brings the two closer together. And most importantly, the perfect guy. The guy who is willing to do absolutely anything for us. Who would change colleges, run after you in the rain, go above and beyond again and again in order to prove the love they have for us. Only... that's not love.

Love is pressing through a fight to remember your love for each other. Love is knowing it's not a guy's job to chase after you, but for you both to pursue each other. We sit around wishing the perfect CW-esc guy would come along and sweep us off of our feet so we can be in a relationship worth bragging about on Instagram. All the while, the good guys get trampled over again and again while we complain about there not being the perfect guy out there.

Guess what? There is no such thing as a perfect guy. But there are a lot of outstanding men who want to chase after someone, but either get passed over or decide not to go for it because they don't see themselves as worth it. We have come to an amazing empowering time in women's history, but that means nothing if we do not bring men with us. In the garden, Eve was taken from the rib of Adam to show equality. To show

86

a partnership. I recognize there is some sexism that happens to women. Trust me, I am not saying it's not there. As a woman who believes she can not only be in leadership, but feels called to preach, I have experienced sexism. In my want for an equal empowerment of people, I recognize that it is not about bringing men down. We need to recognize that our men need empowering, too. Women may have an unrealistic body image to achieve, but men have an unrealistic emotional image to achieve.

Unfortunately, I have seen many good men be led astray to believe they can never achieve what is being expected of them. So they decide to just be the opposite of what is expected. I have also seen men I love, my brother and guys who are like my brother, suffer because they never feel good enough. They feel as though in any relationship if something goes wrong, then it's on them, that it reflects on their heart if they mess up, or if there is any fight, the blame is always on them. If they make the slightest mistake, then they will be labeled as an evil man, so they chose to not take a risk on a relationship. Or when they do, they end up feeling like dirt.

One day, I was talking to one of my married friends about this concept. She had been married for around three years at this point. I can genuinely say that her husband is an outstanding man of God and one of my favorite people. When I was telling her about how I noticed that failure to do something right in a relationship felt like a failure in their character, she paused for a moment. Then told me how she had never thought about it like that, but when she tells her husband he needs to do the dishes or that he forgot to do something she had asked, he would respond with something along the lines of "sorry I am a bad husband." What she meant as a reminder, he took as a failure to her and to his character. As we talked about this, she said, "I thought this was just something he did... I didn't realize it was something going on in most men."

―――――――――

One of my best friends, let's call him Ben, in his senior year of high school, got wrapped up in some drama of sorts with a girl. She imagined this relationship in a much deeper way than he did (they weren't actually dating; they were just friends.) In the end, even though Ben was not in the wrong, he had to take the full responsibility for everything that happened in order to keep peace in the youth group. In conversations I have had with him and other guy friends about this after the situation, they all responded they expect that. They expect to have to take the weight of everything, even if it wasn't their fault.

Ladies, if you want a guy who will treat you like a queen, you need to treat him like a king. I'm not saying that to sound cheesy, I'm saying that because marriage was always meant to be a partnership. So many people want to be treated like a queen while they treat their partners as a jester. You need to accept equal responsibility and pursue each other.

In conversations I have had with some of my younger friends (and I absolutely did this when I was younger) I heard them talk about wanting a big romantic gesture, or they would talk about how mad they were that their significant other had not done anything special in a while. When asked what they have done for their boyfriends recently, it is usually met with a blank stare and eventually a "what do you mean?"

What I mean is, men deserve to be shown love, too. And if we want to see a generation of Christ-like men stepping up to the plate, we have to love them in the way we expect to be loved.

The more guys I talk to, the more I realize that a lot of men genuinely do not know how to help when someone around them is going through something emotional. I propose that there are two main reasons a guy might feel uncomfortable in this kind of situation. The first is because they feel like they need to be the hero in this situation. The second, and what I would say is more likely: because guys are not taught how to manage their own emotions, so how can we expect them to handle other people's?

The current depiction of men in the media makes it basically impossible for a real life guy to come off looking like the guys we dream of. Yet as females, we have this incredibly high expectation for a guy to put in way more effort than we do. We expect them to take steps into boldness while we barely give them the time of day. We say that a real man could ask us out and make his expectations very clear even when we don't show any interest, but cannot recognize that most men have acted boldly and been burned in the past.

I know if I had ever asked out even one person and had been turned down, my confidence would be shaken and I would never do it again. Yet I have, for a lot of my life, held the standard that it shouldn't matter to a guy. He should have the balls to ask me out. It wasn't until one night I was talking to my brother that I began to understand how hard that expectation was. I am not the most expressive person and if I like you, there is no way I am about to let it show. When I was talking to my brother about this guy I had found cute, he asked me if I had shown him any signs of finding him attractive. I said no; I am terrible at flirting. He continued to explain to me how he saw the situation because he has lived his whole life having to be the "bold" person. This conversation began to open my eyes to the unrealistic expectation I was holding men to. I'm not saying that as a female you should have to ask a guy out, but the expectation for a guy to just be bold and do it, even if there are no signs of flirtation, is an absolute double standard.

Manly men

There has been this stronghold for years that says if you are more in touch with your feminine side, then you are automatically assumed to be gay. I hate this stereotype for two reasons. First, I have seen how detrimental it can be to a guy. I am not making any statements about sexual orientation, I just want to say that trying to push someone to be homosexual is just as bad as trying to force someone to be straight. The second reason I hate this stereotype is because it makes men assume they cannot be in touch with their emotions.

There are a few of my male friends who have walked me through what this was like in their lives. Men who are more in touch with their feelings who would constantly be told that they were gay. Which led them to have huge identity challenges. Wondering "maybe I am?" even though they had no feelings towards the same gender. This would go on for years to be something they struggled with because they felt like they were not being accepted for who they were. Which also led them to suppress their emotions, which made things even harder for them.

I won't go into more detail on these because they are not my story to share, but I am sure you can look around your life and find someone with a similar story.

The other reason I hate this stereotype is because it reinforces this idea to men that they should not be in touch with their emotions, which is complete garbage. This is also a double standard that I think we as women can create sometimes because we want men to be emotional for us, but not overly emotional in general. It is vital for us to recognize that showing emotions shouldn't give us assumptions about men, but should just be a normal thing in our lives.

One reason that I believe men struggle at showing emotion is because their emotions get used against them. I think this can happen in several ways. One way is by having their emotions used as a blackmail of sorts, by women or other men telling them they are not "manly" enough or that their problems do not matter. Another way I believe their emotions get used against them is when they tell their female friends/wives/girlfriends about something they are feeling, and end up upsetting them and having to comfort them instead of being able to actually express their feelings. If we want men to start sharing, we have to remember that their feelings are just as valid as ours.

Female roles

The Paradox of being a Woman

Taylor Swift is my absolute favorite artist. I think she is one of the most talented people in music. I grew up listening to her albums. Growing up, I have watched many of the challenges that she has faced and came to realize that life for females is trying to navigate through a series of contradictions. I use Taylor Swift because she was the person I could find this thought easiest to transfer to so that hopefully people understand what I am trying to say.

Taylor Swift was criticized for dating too many people, but I remember reading an article in high school saying that she was a "prude" for not sleeping with her boyfriend. She was constantly criticized for her dating, but those relationships gave relatable content that if she hadn't had, she would have had a different label put on her. Even when she stopped writing about break ups and wrote about other things people were unwilling to get rid of a label they put on her. In reality, I think Taylor has had around 9 boyfriends (that's what the internet said) which I think we can all agree is a perfectly normal number. But the contradictions of being a woman say otherwise. Taylor has had many successful albums over the years and where most people would say she has earned the right to be confident, others say she is too cocky. Her song "The Man" is my favorite song that expresses these contradictions. It shows that it really doesn't matter what you do, people are going to keep their labels on you if that's what they want to do. Taylor Swift still gets negative raps from people even though she writes music people not only relate to, but bond over. I know some of my favorite moments with my friends are jamming out to her songs in the car.

In conclusion, being a woman feels like you can never accomplish what people are asking for. Before I get too deep into this, I want to point out that I am not talking just about expectations men put on us. I think so often when we see stuff like this we automatically assume it is on the other gender, but to be honest with you, the people in my life who I feel create the things I am about to talk about are rarely male. Most of the time, it is other women.

Being a female is a constant process of navigating contradictions that are put on us. Dress modestly so as not to be a whore, but not too modestly, so you are not seen as a prude. You can be a boss babe, but make sure you are not too bossy. You can have big aspirations, just don't be too intimidating.

Essentially, it comes down to the two biggest stereotypes we see of women. On the one side there is the tough, ambitious one who can't show emotion or struggles and who speaks their minds. She is often considered "too much." Then you have the more girly girls who are expected to be more soft tempered. These are the girls that people assume they can walk over and they will go along with anything. It's when these two stereotypes start to crossover that people point things out. I am not just talking about men here, I would say the biggest critics I have had are other women.

Like Taylor, I think that in order to be freed from these things; we have to break ourselves out. We have to be the ones to decide who we want to be and be okay with not being like the rest. I heard someone say once that being a woman is trying to be everything, all the time, and you are not supposed to let anyone see you sweat.

I propose we change that narrative. It's up to us to change the way we see ourselves and other women. Instead of constantly criticizing other women, build them up. Not just those in your close friend group, but all the women you know. There will always be people who are going to criticize you, but I believe that if we as women came together and stopped criticizing each other, we would see more growth than we could ever expect.

Emotional manipulation

The world is full of double standards, and there are many that I could talk about, but this one is my absolute least favorite. I believe that there are plenty of bad stereotypes out there for women right now, but I also think there are some unhealthy ones that we have accepted as things that are okay for women to do that are genuinely terrible things. The biggest example of this is emotional manipulation. If a man is seen emotionally manipulating people, he is immediately cast as the villain, but if a woman does it suddenly she is seen as a boss babe or a hero. Here is one example of what I mean.

Hustlers

The movie Hustlers follows a group of strippers who need extra money. They decide to drug men and rob them in order to make more money. If the roles were reversed, not only would that movie have tanked, but there would have been a massive uproar.

I give this example because I have seen things like this in the real world. I have seen men I love emotionally manipulated by women and then still viewed as the bad guy when they end the relationship. It honestly breaks my heart. I know that the road goes both ways; the difference is that women being gaslighted and emotionally manipulated is talked about constantly.

It is not the same for the men in our lives. I have heard many conversations between people I know where they will talk about something they did in a relationship that is in no way okay, but they then have the backup of their female friends telling them it's okay because he is "just a guy." Then we are shocked when guys become cold and distant or don't talk about their feelings when most guys have experienced their feelings being held against them once they open up.

There are so many stereotypes and character attributes we see in our world. These are just the ones I see most prominently. I encourage you to not just take the ones I have given you, but think of some of your own that you notice and look at how they are impacting society. In order to find out who we are, we have to recognize all the things influencing us, including the media. Once you have sorted that out, I believe we can get a better picture of who God says we are.

Godly Identity

In order to step into the fullness that Christ has for us, we have to trade out the identities we have created in this world for the things that Christ says. To fully cover this topic, I would honestly probably need another book but for now, here's my challenge to you. Find the things in this chapter that you resonate with. The things that you see in your identity that came from the media. Really take a look at your life and see where media and stereotypes have shaped you and then ask God what He has instead of those. This could take time to recognize what God wants to swap out for those things, but I promise if you take the time, He will come through. For example, it could look something like this.

"Sometimes I feel anxious, like I have to wear the weight of the world on my shoulders. That is what I have found in my worldly identity, but God what do you say?" For me, the answer to that anxiety is not a part of me. Instead of anxiety, God says I have been given the Holy Spirit that brings power, love and a sound mind. I no longer feel as though I have to carry the weight of the world on my shoulders, because I know Jesus took that weight for me.

These are the declarations I say over myself when I start to feel anxiety or heaviness. In order to live in Godly identity, we have to recognize what God says, over what the world is saying. The last part of our identity I want to talk about is how we can love how God made us. In a world that pushes an unrealistic sense of beauty and identity, how do we love the person God created instead of wishing for an idea created by the media.

The Beauty Standard

One of the biggest complaints I think we hear about this generation of females is they make themselves look 20 when they are 12. I know for a fact I have said this. I'm not sure why we are surprised by this though when every single teenager portrayed in a drama is played by a person in their 20s. Not even a normal person in their 20s, are a ridiculously beautiful or handsome person who could be a model. When this is how they are being portrayed in the world, why wouldn't we expect them to try to look like that?

It seems like no matter how much we try to create body positivity movements, there are so many people still struggling with self love. This is not just a female issue, I know just as many men who struggle to love their bodies. I believe it is because the places we have targeted are not the highest influences in our lives. Commercials and even social media have changed their beauty standard but the two that have yet to change are film and television.

Any show or movie still has the main characters with the perfect body and a perfect complexion. When they do feature a "plus size" actor, they usually have to rely on their wit to be seen as a contribution to the film. Even at that, the people who are considered "plus size" should really be considered a normal weight. I remember when watching Disney shows as a kid, we were trained to believe that characters like Harper from Wizards of Waverly Place or Raven from That's So Raven were plus sized. When I see those shows now, it makes me furious that the standard for being skinny was so high. If we want to see a genuine change in the beauty standard, then we need to change the most influential source of that standard.

Self-love

I'll never forget the day or the voice of the woman who first told me I was overweight. I was a junior in high school doing my yearly physical. I walked through the halls of our aquatic center, up to a nurse who had me get on a scale. I am 5ft 1in (technically 1¾) and weighed 140 pounds. Which meant that when I hopped up on the scale, she told me that I was overweight. I have a curvier build, and was nowhere near overweight, but in that moment she confirmed every insecure thought that had gone through my head. I wish I had known at that moment that the BMI scale that only goes by height and weight is not super accurate since everyone has different body types, but I am not even sure I would have listened to that. All I heard was that I was fat. Everything I saw on television confirmed that.

Growing up, I think that the last word anyone would have labeled me as was unconfident. I was a little spitfire child who really did not care what anyone thought. I was very secure in my identity with Christ and knew He had called me to do great things. That all changed when I was in eighth grade and encountered a person who was not the kindest of people.

Anytime she saw me, she would make some comment on my physical appearance, whether it was my hair, my clothes, how I looked, anything. It wasn't really what she said that hurt the most; it was that I had friends around at the time who did not contradict what she said. Slowly, without realizing it, I took some of these things into my heart. I took some of these so much to heart that I would realize habits I had in college that started because of comments she would make when I was in eighth grade. As I went into my sophomore year of high school, I became less and less confident on the inside.

In the relationship I mentioned earlier, my self image started fairly high, but continued to get worse and worse as the relationship went on. When I would bring up to him anything about it, he would blow it off or make me feel like I was just doing it to get attention, so I stopped talking about it. Sometimes he would make subtle comments about things that at the time I did not recognize as wrong. For instance, I remember one time being at a pool with him and I was in a bikini. While we were hanging out, he made the comment that one of his friends had asked him something along the lines of "so Ashlee has some love handles, right?" For the record, I had VERY small love handles at the time. After that comment, he said some crap that he didn't notice or didn't care.

The way he said it made him seem like the hero of the moment for not caring that I didn't have a completely flat stomach. It wasn't until later in life that I would come to realize that those small comments he would make were actually manipulative and a reinforcement that I did not have the body that I was supposed to. Comments like that had made me feel like my curves were something to be ashamed of. Every time I looked in the mirror and did not have a completely flat stomach, all I could think of was how fat I was. I would look at other girls who had on perfect makeup, perfect hair and perfect body and would wonder why I couldn't just look like that.

Slowly, and unconsciously, I began hating my outward appearance. Starting in 8th grade and becoming greater and greater until I went to college and still saw myself as unattractive and fat. Throughout college, I would look at other girls and think of how lucky they were to be so pretty and have such nice bodies. It did not matter if people encouraged me or told me I looked good, I could not shake this feeling. I constantly would look back at pictures and be mad at myself because I would realize that I looked good in them, but at the time didn't feel like I did. I would then think to myself I wished I looked like that now. This was a constant cycle. Even times when I was at the exact same weight I was in a picture, I would just think of how much better I looked back then.

I felt so much shame because I thought that since I was a Christian and loved God and knew God loved me, I shouldn't feel this way. I felt as though I was failing the kids I was interning with by not fully loving myself and was telling them to love themselves. I would go through seasons of feeling very confident for a little while and then would end up losing it all for months.

Honestly, this is still a constant struggle for me. I wish I could sit here and tell you that now everything is great and I have full confidence in myself and my body but that would be a lie. I still have plenty of days where I wake up feeling self-conscious and unattractive, but I can tell you that it has gotten much better. I can tell you that at this moment of writing this I am the heaviest I have been, and have found a way to love myself in ways that I never did when I was thinner. While there is still a lot of work I have to do, I want to share just a few things I have learned that can hopefully help you too.

I see posts on Instagram and Facebook all the time of women posting pictures and talking about their journeys and always ending with something like you just need to love yourself and you will feel better! (I am not putting hate on any of these people, I love their heart and journey.) However, I would read those and think how? How do I get to love myself? It's not just a switch that I can flip on, like some people made it seem. I felt at a loss to not know how to begin this journey and did not want to ask people around me because I thought they wouldn't understand or would see me as weak or would just tell me that I am beautiful. We all need to hear that, but it doesn't matter how many times you hear it if you do not believe.

Slowly, and I mean very slowly, I found things that helped me. The first was truly recognizing the Father's love for me. Once I fully let that in, I saw everything about myself in a new way. But even with that, I still look in the mirror or at pictures and not like what I see, and I would still see myself as significantly heavier than I was. Here are a few things that have helped me on my journey to loving my outward self more.

1. Prayer

This was what I would say was the most important part of transforming my mind. Anytime that I would see a picture of myself I didn't like or would see myself in the mirror, I would ask the Lord to give me eyes to see myself the way that He and other people see me. I prayed this prayer constantly (and still do). Anytime I felt insecure, I would go to the Father instead of people on media. Suddenly, my eyes changed. I saw myself as curvy, not fat. I saw the beauty that lit up my smile, the love that was carried through my eyes, the joy carried through my laugh. I looked in the reflection and would smile, not drive my mind crazy with everything that was wrong. I could see the curves of my body and recognize their beauty without wishing that I had a different frame or a smaller stomach. I saw what the Lord saw. I saw beauty. The most important advice I could give you is to pray. Anytime that voice tells you that you are not enough or aren't fearfully and wonderfully made, pray for God's eyes instead of your own. It may not happen automatically, but with time, I believe you will notice a difference in what you see.

2. Compliment yourself

We become what we think about most. So if we only are giving hatred to ourselves and thinking negatively about who we are, then that is all we will see. A simple shift can change that. I encourage you, whenever you look in the mirror and start thinking negatively, stop your thoughts and say two things you like about yourself. It may feel really hard and uncomfortable at first, but eventually it will become easier. Eventually, you will find a point where you can list more than two things. Switch your mind to see the positives of your body, not the negatives. Train your mind in the same way you would train your body.

3. Don't be afraid of affirmation

This was the hardest thing for me to put into my life. I know I said compliments could not change the way I saw myself, but sometimes you need other people's affirmation. Our worth cannot be built solely on that. First, we have to fix our mind so that we actually receive compliments and don't just write them off. After I started making the internal shift, I utilized things I had with the community around me. Warning: this will feel very uncomfortable. Whenever I felt very insecure and could not get myself out of it, I would ask a friend to tell me what they liked about my physical appearance that day. Whatever they said, I would take that to heart. I would not write it off like I used to and think they were just being polite, but I would truly cherish it.

Chapter Eight:

Social Media Identities

We form so much of our identities based on social media. Who is following us, how many likes someone gets, what someone else's life looks like. We have trained ourselves to look at social media as the best way to judge someone's life. Making it on TikTok is now what it means to make it in the world. Having thousands of likes feeds our egos and makes us feel worthy. What we always forget is that people's lives on social media are not their life. It is the version of their life that they want everyone else to see. We get so caught up in trying to compare our lives to these "perfect" versions of someone else's life we end up losing sight of what is real. We compare our worth to the perfect picture of someone.

I have seen influencers take their pictures; I promise you it is not something they just took a snapshot of. It is something they took multiple photos with different angles, different filters, different backgrounds, and so many other things. Even on TikTok, when you make a video, it has the enhanced ability to make your face look flawless. When all you do is use features like that, I can all but guarantee that you will start disliking yourself in the mirror. Those are not real, but we take them on as a very real part of our identity. It's hard not to. It is hard to not want to compare yourself to the influencers you see, but we have to remind ourselves that what people show on social media is not always true. If we try forever to make our lives, look like those we see on our phones, we miss the real beauty in ourselves and in the world around us. We have created this culture that puts influencers on a high pedestal, but I think we have lost sight of what the word influence even means.

Before we get too deep into this, I want to ask you a few questions. Take a few minutes to ponder what your answers are to each of these.

1. When you hear the word influence, what comes to mind?

2. On a scale of 1-10 how much influence would you say you have?

3. Other than your parents, who are the three people who have had the most influence on who you are as a person?

Our world view of influence has been set askew. I think in order for us to recognize the influence we actually have over people; we need to recognize the worldview of what influence is, and what real and biblical influence looks like.

We have a very messed up view of what influence actually looks like. We spend so much time chasing after what the world sees as influence, and honestly I believe that leaves a lot of us feeling empty. What the world sees as influence is unattainable for most people. I know I get stuck all the time striving for worldly influence that it can cause me to miss the influence I do have.

We look at the followers we have or don't have or how many likes we have on videos and we obsess over those numbers so much that we forget about the people that matter. The world tells us that influence is about width. The prettier you are, the more deserving of influence you are. We attribute influence and leadership to the funniest or loudest people. Just because you have a platform does not mean you have influence. Influence is the ability to change people. To change their thoughts, their character, their actions, their perception. We chase this dream of being widely known, but even if we achieve that dream, you probably won't be fulfilled.

I have struggled with my perception of influence for a long time. I've always felt like I did not have any influence. If I walk in a room, I'm not the loudest or most outgoing. I am not the person people are immediately drawn to or the one who gets given opportunities without even asking. I have based part of my identity on that for so long. Thinking that because of those things I wasn't very influential. I based my idea of influence on how popular I was or based it on what I saw in the mirror, because honestly I based a lot of my influence on how I looked. One day, I went out to a camp that a lot of my past students were at. I went to hear one of my friends give a seminar and she talked about how a lot of times as women sometimes we take our worth or our ability to do things to be directly linked to our looks.

It was a concept I had heard many times before, but that day there was something new that stood out to me this time. She focused a little more on the fact that we as people will often attribute not just our worth, but our abilities to the way we look. This concept was what stuck with me that day. Recognizing that my looks, my social media and my perception did not change the influence I had. What I would notice that day is a group of girls that I had known for a few years who were immensely excited to see me. Excited to update me on their lives, boys, camp, school and everything in between.

If I hadn't heard my friend's seminar that day I am not sure that I would have noticed this, but on my drive home the Lord started speaking to me about my influence. About how in those moments, those girls couldn't care less that I had gained weight, or that I wasn't what the world would consider influential. They wanted to be around me because of the time I invested in their lives.

I began to realize that the things I looked at as influence were not completely accurate. I would now argue that the person that has the most influence is not the person who is the loudest in the room but the one who is quickest to listen. Influence isn't about how many people can hear you. It's about how many people are willing to change when they hear what you have to say.

What can we see in scripture about influence?

In all honesty, I think if Jesus were alive today, He would have a lot of people hate on the way He did ministry. Not on the miracles or teachings, but on the fact that He chose to spend more time with His smaller community groups than He did with the crowds. I believe most people would have judged Him by thinking that He was wasting His time with smaller groups when He had the crowds. I believe that this was very intentional. What we can learn from the way Jesus used His influence is that influence is about depth. Not width.

You can have thousands of followers on social media and have less influence than someone with one. If Jesus had only spoken to the crowds, I fully believe that His impact would have been small. Most of us would think that the more people you have access too, the more impact you have. The life of Jesus shows us that it's the relationships that create real, sustainable change. I am not saying to ignore the crowds; I am saying we need to remember that our deepest influence is the people closest to us.

Too often in life we find ourselves striving to have more influence over the crowds and forget about those closest to us. This isn't just on social media. This concerns friend groups too. We can get caught up in wanting to be the person who has the most friends and forget that impact is left by the deeper relationships. I believe we have separated community and influence when those things should go hand in hand. Our community should be our deepest source and form of influence.

104

The world has put influencers and stars on a pedestal, but in reality, influencers may impact trends but that does not mean that they impact lives. I'm not saying they have no influence over people, but when I look at my life, there is not a single influencer or movie star that I would put anywhere close on my list of influential people in my life. The people who have really changed my life, the way I act, the way I see the world, everything, are the people who invested time in me, not people I just see on a screen. Yet we still chase being an "influencer". Real influence is shaping people. Not culture.

We have created this mindset that says the more followers/friends you have, the more value you have. That is so far from the truth. Your worth is not contingent on your followers or friends.

We spend so much of our lives envying other people on social media. Whether we envy their following, their spouse, their kids, whatever it is, we spend too much time wanting the "perfect" life we see others have on social media. We get so wrapped up in our favorite TikTokers or movie stars that we do not even realize the influence we have over others. At the beginning of this chapter I asked how much influence you believe you have. For everyone, I think the real answer is the same. It depends. It depends on the relationship. There are people in my life where I would say my influence is a 10. There are other people where I would say a 1. We have to remind ourselves that influence is about relationships.

I know personally I tend to forget that I carry influence. Probably much more than I realize. That night at church camp I mentioned earlier was when the realization of my influence hit. That realization changed so much for me. It made me more aware of those around me and helped me to bring my focus to those who I already had in my life who were being influenced by the things I did. It made me stop caring about the width of my reach and want to really pour in and pay more attention to the reach I already had. Everyone has people in their life who watch them. Even if you do not realize it. It could be someone at church, work, school, wherever there are people you have influence. If we are always thinking about how much wider we want our influence to be, then we end up missing the influence we have.

Influence in ministry

This worldly idea of influence has slipped into our churches as well. Too often we get caught up in the numbers game. The question becomes how many people are at our events, rather than what impact are we leaving? I love big worship nights and camps, but in all honesty the people who have shaped my life are the people who have discipled me. The people who have taken the time to invest in my life and what I am doing. I think we have lost focus on this as a church. We focus more on getting hundreds of people into the church building, but then have no discipleship when discipleship is what brings change.

Discipleship

I believe discipleship may be one of the most overlooked aspects of the church today. The majority of Jesus' time in scripture shows how He discipled people every single day, yet most of us think it is a suggestion or something that is meant only for people in ministry. You can see the concept of discipleship throughout scripture, but so many of us decide not to do it. Change comes from discipleship. It is not something that is only meant for people who work in ministry. It is something everyone in the church should be doing.

We spend so much time as church staff trying to plan events that hundreds of people will come to, and we forget the importance of one-on-one relationships. If you have thousands of people coming to your services but no discipleship, I truly believe you need to take a look at the way your ministry is run. Ministry is not a numbers game. It's about the one.

The
Meet
Cute

Chapter Nine:

Epic Love Stories

Romeo and Juliet. Jack and Rose. Cinderella and Prince Charming. I could go on and on with names of epic love stories. Stories that make your heart yearn for the love that is experienced by characters in our beloved stories. The love that makes people risk their lives to save that other person. The type of love that leaves everything else behind for that one person. The type of love that everyone yearns for in life. Love stories that seem slightly out of reach. Love stories that have created a misconception of love.

We have entered a time where people build relationships based on fantasy. With unrealistic expectations and sometimes impossible ideas. In a world where fifty percent of marriages end in divorce, most ways we are learning about what relationships look like are through the shows and movies that we watch regularly. Relationships that revolve around drama, unrealistic expectations, and very little about what actually makes a relationship work.

In Bianca Olthoffs sermon series The Miseducation of Love, she describes the metanarrative of love stories so perfectly that I dare not try to come up with my own because I love hers so much. She states that the metanarrative of romantic movies (she is talking specifically about Titanic, but I think it crosses to most films) is "Fall in love after three days, shag whenever you want, make promises you can't keep." I think that is the perfect description of romance movies, and is a perfect example of what we see relationships looking like.

Media subconsciously affects how we view relationships to where we feel as though we need drama in order to have a relationship. In most shows and movies that portray relationships, there is usually some scene where the boy and girl get into a fight about something and both react in an exaggerated way. Some common occurrences are the guy messing up somehow, the girl storming in on the guy and his friends and causing a scene, a dramatic exit, etc. After the dramatic scene, the couple usually gets back together and is stronger than ever. This leaves the impression in our brain that when I am dramatic, it brings us closer. For females specifically, it can cause the idea that when I am dramatic, I get attention/affection. RomComs and shows give us this narrative that this is what qualifies as "epic love." We then spend so much time trying to find our own epic love stories. When we spend so much time looking for "epic love" you may just miss out on authentic love.

It's easy to fall in love with people we see on our screens. From TikTok, to Instagram to our favorite shows, it's easy to fall in love with them because they are not real. They are a perfect version of what we want. They are the perfect body, perfect personality, perfect job, perfect version of what we believe to be a "good person." Of course we fall in love with them so easily. Of course it gives us too high of standards for people we date or for our own love stories. However, the older I get and the longer I have been single the more I recognize I don't want those perfect people. I want real. I don't want the stories I see on screen; I want a guy who looks at me the way my dad still looks at my mom. I don't want epic. I want authentic.

Media gives us this idea that when you are in a relationship, the other person will gain some kind of sixth sense that tells them exactly what you need when you need it. As much as we wish it were true, there is no magical sixth sense that comes out when you enter a relationship, but I believe you can grow in this "sixth sense" through a very simple, yet so complex thing: communication. Even with communication, no one will ever know exactly what you need when you need it. If our parents cannot determine exactly what you need anytime you need something, our significant others definitely cannot.

People say it all the time: communication is essential to healthy relationships. We can say that all we want, but it doesn't matter if we are not living it out. If you just expect your significant other to know exactly what you need at the moment you need it, you will be gravely disappointed. In order to get your needs met, you need to voice your needs. With time, I think these things become second nature in a relationship, but there is no chance for it to happen if you do not voice them. This is true with any relationship.

Media tropes

There are so many tropes that we see in the media, especially in RomComs and in teen dramas. I want to mention a few that I feel are having the biggest impact on our dating culture and how we view romantic relationships.

Romantic gestures fix everything

I experienced firsthand how untrue this is. This has become one of my least favorite things to see in shows. We all know how it goes. The guy and the girl get in a huge fight and then the guy makes some huge romantic gesture to show his "real feelings" and suddenly life is fixed and the relationship is perfect. I have grown to dislike this for a few reasons, most of which I covered in the male and female roles of the previous chapter. The other reason I hate this trope is because it gives the idea that a grand gesture is some sort of magic spell to fix a relationship.

A grand gesture is not a fix all for a relationship. In too many movies, there is a grand gesture that magically fixes things. After the gesture, their differences or fights are not addressed, it is just magically better.

I was re-watching Pitch Perfect while writing this, a movie in which I usually love the ending, but this time I noticed something a little different. There is literally no work put into their relationship being fixed. She proves she finished watching a movie and enjoyed it, so she sang the ending song and then BOOM she fixed all of her emotional problems and somehow magically fixed her relationship with Jesse? Unfortunately, this is the expectation so many people have in real life. They have this expectation that not only will there be a big romantic gesture, but that the gesture will fix everything. I believe this leads to a great deal of heartbreak and lost relationships.

It makes relationships seem too easy. I encourage you, take a break after reading this chapter and go watch your favorite RomCom and see how many of these things fit in it. Then I encourage you to take a very honest look at your own love life and see if you fit any of the expectations set by what you are watching. Then take a few moments to see if those expectations are healthy or if they could be masquerading as romance when it is really toxic.

My parents have been married for over 30 years now. I know without a doubt in my mind that my parents are in love. In that 30 years of marriage, I have never seen my mom dramatically exit a room or do anything dramatic when in a fight. I know for a fact that if my mom acted as a lot of women do in movies, my dad would not go running after her, nor would he make some insanely grand gesture to ask for her forgiveness, he would sit in his chair confused and probably frustrated until he went to bed. My dad is an amazing man. Anytime I see him with my mom, I can tell that he is unconditionally in love with her. The reason I believe their marriage has been so successful is because they do not rely on big gestures. Instead, they daily show each other love. It is not all on my dad, my mom does it too.

It's not about the big romantic gestures, it's about how you show the other person daily that you love them. Grand gestures are great, but if you use them every time you get in a fight, you never get that depth in a relationship that comes with conflict. You will also always be using a temporary fix because no matter how grand the gesture, the problems will always come back if you don't fix them at their root.

I have always looked up to my parents and have wanted the marriage that they have, which made it even more confusing why I would act so dramatically in a relationship rather than to have a healthy mode of communication. The portrayal of relationships in the media sets many unrealistic expectations in our minds, one of which is that when I am overly dramatic, a guy is going to go out of his way to make sure things are set straight. This is an extremely toxic and unfair expectation. I encourage you, next time you watch a romantic movie, watch the big fight scene, and then see how the guy makes up for it. Then really take the time to ask yourself, do I have that expectation for the people in my life? Or maybe for you, you get stuck in the idea that everything that goes wrong in a relationship is something you have to fix. Instead of feeling like you need to fix things together. Whatever it is, I encourage you to really sit down and think through all the aspects of this idea of romantic gestures and see how they fit into your relationship ideology.

A house built on lies

One of the most common themes in media with relationships is lying. Relationships that start out with a lie, have lies in the middle or end with lies. There are so many themes that fall into this category, which I believe has made lying something that people have deemed acceptable as long as it is in the name of romance. Here are a couple examples of what I mean.

Fake dating

To All the Boys I've Loved Before is the perfect example of this. The story where the couple starts fake dating to make other people jealous but then ends up falling in love with each other. I have literally heard of zero situations in real life where this has happened. I think this puts the idea in people's heads that if they can get someone to pretend to date them, then they will end up together, but in reality, I can only see this leading to heartbreak.

Fake identities

This also ties into the idea of lying about your identity at the start of your relationship. In most cases, if you heard about this happening in real life you would probably consider it a red flag, yet when we watch it in romance movies we find ourselves rooting for the couple. While we may still consider this a red flag, I believe it is a red flag that is commonly ignored.

From *Alladin* to *How to Lose a Guy in 10 Days*, this idea is seen throughout cinema. It runs the idea that if you are lying about who you are, as long as it is for a good reason, you can still make the relationship work. Any relationship that starts out with a lie is not built on healthy foundations. In real life, it might look something like lying about religion, your job or even your age. In any circumstances, relationships need to be built on truth.

Get the makeover, get the guy

From She's All That to D.U.F.F., there are way too many movies and shows out there that run this theme. If you change your appearance, you can have the guy you want. I recognize that in most of the movies that run this idea, the guy ends up falling for the "authentic" version of them, but they fall in love AFTER they have gone through their transformation. This idea gives the impression that you need to change your appearance in order to get the person you have dreamt of, but that eventually they will fall in love with your personality. I have noticed myself falling into this trope all the time. On the days when I am struggling with being single, I usually immediately feel self-conscious and assume that people just must not find me attractive.

Forbidden love

This might be one of the oldest tropes of romance. *Romeo and Juliet, West Side Story and High School Musical* are three of my favorites, but this storyline just promotes the idea that falling in love should be your number one priority and once you do, everyone in your life then becomes expendable.

These examples of movies give off the idea that it is okay to betray everyone you know if it is for love. It is perfectly fine to put your family and friends at risk as long as you are doing it for the love of someone you have known for less than a week.

Destructive love

I can think of no better example of this than Chuck and Blair from *Gossip Girl*. From the beginning, their relationship is in chaos. It is filled with betrayal, backstabbing, and destruction. I'll admit, I love them, but when you look at their relationship, you notice all the incredibly toxic behaviors that are deemed okay in the name of love.

Not only do they destroy each other, but they destroy those around them. They live life as though it is only their relationship that matters. They give this idea that as long as you are doing it together; it is deemed romantic. Instead, it should be seen for what it really is: self-centered and narcissistic. If you believe that your relationship can destroy other people just because you want to, you need to look at how you are viewing yourself and the world around you.

Mismatched couples

I know the saying is opposites attract, but that saying only goes so far. In reality, you need your significant other to be someone with the same values and morals as you do. The most common example I can think of this is in Hallmark movies. These movies constantly show a prominent business woman or overworked person who ends up falling in love with the down to earth, hometown boy. These stories may seem sweet, but if you have a relationship where one person cares more about work and the other cares more about friends and family, you are likely to enter a doomed relationship.

This also can be said for giving an unrealistic expectation for who you have the potential for a date. For instance, in movies about dating someone famous or excessively wealthy, it can put the idea in young girls' heads that they will someday end up with someone famous or very wealthy. I'm not saying this can't happen, it is just rare. It can also put wrong ideals for what you should be looking for in a spouse. It is not about fame and money, but about how well they are suited to each other and how well you can love one another.

Tragic love stories

Over the last few years, I have noticed a trend in romantic movies. There has become this new genre for tragic love stories. Stories where someone in the couple gets in a car accident and almost dies or gets cancer and so on and so forth. While I think love stories like this in real life are beautiful and I am not by any means trying to say they are not real, I think we are coming to where we are romanticizing the idea of tragedy. Where instead of that being something we pray never happens to us, it is now something people are seeing as romantic and strengthening in a relationship. This trend scares me. I think that if we do not change something, then we will see people who believe tragedy is a relationship fixer. That it is something to bring together and strengthen love, rather than what it really is, which is a challenge that could pull couples apart.

Imagine a young girl in an unstable relationship. A relationship where she cares more about the guy than he does her. Now imagine that this girl has seen many movies where a tragedy is a love story, where someone almost dying brings a couple into this dream-like relationship. Now imagine what would happen if her mind began to wander about what would happen if a tragedy happened in her own relationship... If just maybe she was in a terrible accident and went into a coma, he would realize what he has and would love her so much more. I believe that there are already people out there who sometimes have these thoughts, and I pray we never see the day when someone would act on that feeling in a desperate act to fix their relationship or feel something deeper. Although, I would not be surprised if something like this had already happened.

Romanticizing tragedy is a mistake. I think the stories are beautiful when I meet a couple who have been through something like that, but what the movies don't show you is the strain that it puts on relationships. They do not show you the realistic, unromantic, down and dirty parts of tragedy. I know someone who has a story very similar to A Walk to Remember, and I guarantee he would not wish that on anyone. I also know just as many couples who have been torn apart by tragedies rather than brought together. What the movies don't show us is the raw fights and long nights, days of wanting to give up and significantly harder times. I believe that putting these ideas in the minds of young people who are looking for love gives them an inaccurate depiction of what it looks like going through tragedies with someone you are dating or married to.

These stories are beautiful, but we need to be careful of romanticizing the idea of tragedy. When I was in a relationship in high school, things got pretty rough towards the end. I became a person who I no longer recognized. Someone who stayed with a guy after he tried cheating on her, someone who let herself be treated like she was worthless. It was in those times that my brain went to places that I hate thinking about, because had I been a different person, raised by different parents, not in the right community, things could have ended differently.

I remember one time in particular when the guy I had been dating had told me he had feelings for someone else, and my first thought was how can I get him to only want me? Ladies and gents, if this ever happens to you while you are dating, please leave the relationship. Anyway, I remember one day as I was driving there was this little voice in my head that thought maybe if my car crashed and I was a little injured, he would recognize what we have and pull his head out of his butt. Luckily, I was raised by amazing parents and had a great community and would never have done something like that, but the fact is the thought popped into my head. Which means it has probably popped into other people's minds. I worry that for people who were not in the same environment as me, that they may follow that thought down a dangerous path. I know for a fact that had I done something like that, yes, it probably would have pulled him back in for a little (as it would most decent human beings) but it would be temporary. It would not be real.

Christian dating tropes

When I ended the relationship with my high school boyfriend, I made a promise to God. I promised Him I would not date anyone else until He gave me the okay. In my head I thought "I'll take a few months to heal, and then I will meet the love of my life and we will probably be married by the end of college." I have never been so wrong in my life. At this moment, I am in my seventh year of being single. I have learned so much about who God is during that time and it has been absolutely amazing. During this time, I have also had the opportunity to observe what dating looks like in the Christian realm. I have noticed some themes that also come from Christian dating expectations.

While there are many themes we see in romance movies, I think it is also important that we look at how romance is portrayed in Christian culture. I think it is important to be aware of each of these so that you can have the knowledge in your head to recognize when your brain is leaning towards one or the other. First, I want to talk about what singleness looks like in Christian dating culture.

You need to be mentally and physically single

This was something I really did not know was a problem until I was struggling with it. It's easy to tell when you are not physically single. You may not be in a relationship, but if you are constantly going around making out with people, you are not fully physically single. The same thing goes with our minds. If you are constantly making up relationships in your head, you are not living in the fullness of being single. If you are in a season of being single, you need to be fully single to get the full amount of what God has in store for you.

This was something that was hard for me to wrap my mind around until a few years into being single. I would lose myself in fantasies of what a relationship could look like. Whether that was with a boy I knew or a boy I saw on my television screen. For example, Harry Styles, Tom Holland, Archie Andrews, or Damon Salvatore. Or for others, the list may look a little more like Zendaya, Scarlett Johansson or Margot Robbie.

About three years in, I felt a push from the Lord to look deeper into that. I realized I was missing out on so much time that I could have been growing with the Lord, but I was too busy living in this fantasy world. Once I broke that cycle, I noticed a much deeper connection with the Lord because I was actually living single.

If we are constantly creating potential futures in our heads, it not only can create an unknown expectation for someone when you do start dating, but it also keeps us from living in the moment. It continuously keeps us living in the future. When we stop fantasizing what could be, we start to see what God has in store for that time.

Being a single Christian

Through the last few years of singleness, I have had an amazing opportunity to grow with God and also observe how Christian dating culture works. There are few things that I have noticed over the years of being single that I think are important to recognize when we talk about what romance looks like in our culture. I believe that the media influences this a lot, but I also believe Christian culture has a significant influence over how Christians date. These are some things that I have learned through these past years.

Singleness is about being "ready" for a relationship

When I was newly single, the most common thing I would hear was "you will find him when you are ready". Well first, that is a kind of subtle brag insinuating that married people have reached a better place in life and were "ready" to get married. One thing that I heard more times than I can count was, "Don't worry! There's a light at the end of the tunnel!" Giving this idea that I was in a tunnel just waiting for my husband. You hear it all the time whenever somebody gives you advice or tries to comfort you about being single they always say something around the lines of don't worry you're going to find your person when you're ready or when it's "your time." When I was processing being single for so long I always had this thought that I wasn't in a relationship because I wasn't ready.

For some amount of time, I would say that might have been true. I had some things I needed to work on, but after a couple of years I thought: how am I still not ready? Am I just that rough of a person that it is going to take me years to be ready to be in a relationship? One day, while I was processing this with the Lord, I realized that being single right now has nothing to do with my spouse.

Yes, I am becoming the person who Christ made me to be and my husband will benefit from that, but it is in no way about being "ready" for my husband. There have been so many things that I've accomplished in my life since I've been single that I know I couldn't have done if I had been in a relationship. For example, I know that I never would have moved to California or New York, which means I may have never started writing this book or been given the opportunities to preach the gospel.

We hear it all the time, "just wait, there's a light at the end of the tunnel." But in saying this, are we making it our end game to get married? That's not my endgame. I had to come to realize that God had so much more planned for me and the reason I was single actually had nothing to do with me being "ready." It had everything to do with what the Lord was calling me to in those moments.

This mindset also creates this idea in our minds that when we are single, we are just working on getting ourselves ready so that we can be with our spouse. After about two years of being single, I doubted this idea of being single because I wasn't "ready." Emotionally and spiritually, I think I could have been in a relationship a while ago. The reason I was single had nothing to do with not being ready and everything to do with God's plan. What He had planned for me was something I needed to do alone. One of the biggest perks of being single is that you can solely focus on Christ. That meant when God told me to move to New York, I did it with zero hesitation. I got confirmation and started making plans to move. Something that is harder to do when you have a spouse and kids. I think so many of us can miss what God is calling us to when we are single because we are stuck thinking that the reason we are single is that we are becoming who we need to be for our spouse.

Hearing this idea all the time gave me this feeling that I was not good enough to be in a relationship. When you go in with that mindset, it sets your mind to think I am not good enough to be in a relationship now, but I might be in the future.

The light isn't at the end of the tunnel, it's in the tunnel with us. And that light is not our spouse, it's Jesus. When we view our future spouse as the "light" that will suddenly make our life brighter, we are putting them in the place where Jesus is meant to be. Instead, I like to think that there's a light in the tunnel with me, and eventually my future spouse and I will walk together in the light.

My spouse will benefit from the growth I have done over the last few years, but it is not for him. It is for the Kingdom and the glory of God. I am becoming who God has called me to be, not the person my future spouse needs.

Seasons of singleness

One trend I see in Christian culture is this idea of a season of singleness. I believe this topic is something that needs to be talked about more, but in a more real sense. The fact is that a season of singleness is a new thing. Until about a hundred years ago, there was no option to have a season where you could be single. Especially as women. I believe that sometimes we look at the time of singleness as such a burden because we feel as though we need to be married by a certain age and we end up missing how much of a blessing it actually is to get to be single for a time. We now get the opportunity to go however long we want to be single and focus purely on God and what He has for us, and who He has called us to be. I believe that if we stopped idolizing marriage and thinking that is our end goal, we would recognize everything that we have available to us.

That being said, what I am about to say might contradict a little, but I think it is important to mention. Not everyone who is single is meant to be in a season of singleness. I believe that sometimes we use that idea as an excuse to not actually put ourselves out there and date. If you feel a grace from the Lord to date, then I firmly believe that you should date. If you want to get married, you have to date. There are so many stigmas with Christian dating, some of which I will get into, but I believe we need to be aware of if we are actually being called into a season of singleness or if we are using it as an excuse.

I find it so interesting that this is the only aspect of Christianity where the most common advice is to do nothing. Just wait, and your person will find you. If neither of you are looking, it will be pretty hard to find each other. In every other aspect of our faith, we tell people that they need to take action. You want a deeper understanding of God, read more scripture. If you want to pastor, go to seminary. Yet for some reason, when it comes to dating we always tell people to just wait until their time comes. I believe if you want to get married and feel a grace from the Lord, you should date. With that, I think there are some common Christian dating themes we have to recognize so that we can date well.

Dating stigmas

In order to create a culture where Christians can date well, we have to get rid of the stigma that goes with dating. I'm not sure why, but I know that for most Christians when they do try to date there is this embarrassment of sorts that comes with it. This sense of embarrassment that makes it feel as though it is something you cannot talk about because others will judge you. If we want to get married, why shouldn't we date? I am not sure exactly where this stigma comes from, but I know that it is felt by many Christians, especially after you graduate college. I know for me personally, the idea of telling someone that I was on a dating app or was trying to date, feels so embarrassing. It feels almost shameful. I have never been able to fully put my finger on why, but I believe that it is something we have to change if we want to see a healthy dating culture.

High stakes dating

One reason I believe that there is a rising number of Christians not getting married is because we have created a high stakes dating environment. Basically, what that means is we have created a culture where if you are going to go to coffee or a first date with someone, then you have to see yourself marrying that person. Which usually causes people to wait an insane amount of time to ask someone out and they end up either missing their opportunity or getting put in the friend zone.

I am convinced that one of the reasons we see people in the "friend zone" or missing opportunities to date is actually very simple. I think as females we tend to catch feelings quickly. When we first meet a guy or have known him for just a little bit we may start to have a crush on him. But after a few months go by, we lose it. For guys, even if they do have feelings at the beginning, I think that the high stakes dating culture makes them want to wait until they are more sure, which leads to ending up in the "friend zone."

We need to lower the stakes of dating. We have to recognize that going on one date is not a life or death situation. It can purely be a "Hey, you're cute and fun to be around. Let's see if there is something more between us." Along with this, we have to learn how to say no to second dates if we are not feeling it. This is one that I would struggle with because I hate hurting people's feelings.

When I was a sophomore in college, I was convinced that I was ready to date. I was just waiting for the Lord to send me a guy. Towards the end of that year, one of my close guy friends asked me out. Immediately I had the same feeling from the Lord as I did when I started my relationship in high school: I was supposed to say no. Some events transpired and after some push from friends, I said yes. Even though I knew with everything inside of me I was not supposed to. For the next two days, I was racked with guilt until I finally called off the date. In order to lower the stakes of dating, we have to get rid of this people pleasing mentality to say yes even if we do not see it going anywhere.

I am not saying that you should not have marriage in mind when you are in a relationship. I wholeheartedly believe that you should. What I am saying is that marriage does not have to be on your mind on your first or second date. It's okay to go on a date and it not work out. For so many of us Christians we feel as though a failed date makes me look like a failure or that I am doing something wrong.

In order to create a healthy dating culture I believe two things are absolutely necessary. First, we have to lower the stakes of dating. We have to recognize that you do not need to know you are getting married on the first date. Second, we have to get rid of the stigma of dating. We need to create environments that say it is okay to go on dates, be on dating apps and most importantly, fail at dating. Not every date will lead to marriage, but if you do not go on any dates, you are way less likely to have something lead to marriage.

Are you waiting on a God moment or a movie moment?

The most important factor in this is that we need to be listening to what God is saying. If God is telling you to be completely single, do that, but if you feel a release from the Lord saying you can date, then you should do that. We just have to learn to do it differently.

As I mentioned, I have been single for the last few years. In my head, I had made up this idea that when I was supposed to get married, God would somehow just throw a man into my life, RomCom style. For example, I would dream that one day while I was at a coffee shop, I would spill my drink and a very attractive, God-loving man would help me clean it up. Then we would talk for hours until it would lead to a date. While I believe God can work that way, I was not dreaming it from my relationship with Christ; I was dreaming it because of my love for movies.

While I was writing this, I felt like the Lord was saying that soon I would be able to date. I was a little confused, so I asked the Lord why I would date when I trust He would make it happen? It was in that moment that I heard so clearly the Lord say, "You are not waiting on a God moment, you are waiting on a movie moment." For years, I had been stuck with this idea that I would have this movie like connection with someone instead of really listening to what God was saying. When He started this process in my heart, I still felt called to be single, but I could feel Him preparing my heart to date.

We have to be able to separate Godly expectations from movie expectations. When we go in expecting a movie moment, you may miss your God moment.

What is love?

From both of these ends of the spectrum, we have very different narratives being taught. On one end, we are being told that you can date whoever, whenever you want. On the other, we are being told not to date unless you think they are who you will marry. Unfortunately, dating has only been around for the last few decades, which means that sometimes it can be harder to find scripture on what dating should look like. What we do have is scriptures of what love should look like. What romance between a husband and wife should be.

In case you were wondering about some of the differences, I made a table that goes through 1 Corinthians 13. This is one of the most quoted wedding scriptures. Next to the things the scriptures say about love, I put what the media says about love. In order to have the romance we want, we need to go to scripture. Not the media.

Biblical: 1 Cor. 13	Media
Patient	Moody
Kind	Can be harsh
Does not envy	Jealous
Does not boast	Should brag
Is not arrogant or proud	Filled with pride
It does not dishonor others	Dishonors people who disagree
It does not insist on its own way	It's my way or the highway
Is not easily angered	Hot tempered
Is not resentful	Holds grudges
Does not rejoice at wrongdoings/keeps no record of wrongs	Holds onto wrongdoings to throw in your face when it is convenient
Does not delight in evil, but rejoices in the truth	Makes situations morally gray
Always protects	Is protective
Always trusts	Trust is earned, not free
Always hopes	Loses hope as quickly as its gained
Always perseveres	Gives up when it's too hard or too inconvenient

With both ends of the spectrum telling us different things, we have to be sure we are rooted in what scripture says. As dating is a fairly new thing, it can be frustrating trying to navigate what it is supposed to look like. In order to date well, you need to be focused on your relationship with Christ. Know what you are looking for in a spouse, not on a checklist, more of attributes you know they need to have. Then partner with God to see where you are at. Have conversations with those around you to see what they think. Too often in Christian culture we try to do everything alone, but communities and the people discipling us can also play a crucial role in so many other aspects of life. Stop looking for a movie and start searching for a God moment.

Chapter Ten:

The Sexual Agenda

Desensitization

We have become desensitized to seeing sex. What used to be considered extremely risque and inappropriate is now considered completely normal on television. I went to watch Marvels The Eternals while writing this and was shocked by the sex scene in the movie. What shocked me the most was how casual most people were about it. I began having conversations with more and more people about it, and most of them did not even think about it. They saw it as no big deal, but I just could not let this go.

I had seen much worse scenes on shows, so why was this one so different? It was at that moment that it hit me just how far we had come to being desensitized by sex. I was sitting in a movie with kids that could not have been more than 10 years old watching this scene and all I could think was, how is this so normal? If I saw that same scene in a television show I was watching, it wouldn't have bothered me because I expect it now in basically any show I watch. But I was so distressed because it felt like the movies that I had always seen as family-friendly movies now felt inappropriate.

Everyone else around me was unphased. Honestly, the only reason I was phased was that the Lord has put this topic on my heart so strongly and I was in the middle of writing this book, so everything was fresh in my mind. We have to change the narrative. Having a scene in what is considered a family movie where you can see a man thrusting should be a sign that we need to be more vigilant about just how far our culture has gone from sexual purity. Imagine for a second that scene replaced the sex scene in Iron Man? Do you think Marvel would have ended up as big as it is today? I don't. While that was only a few years ago, the standard for sexual content was significantly different.

We are living in a sexually immoral culture and right now we are turning away hoping that the problem goes away on its own. I know this topic is hard to address and there are going to be things in this chapter that may feel offensive or hard to hear, but I would rather address these now and help people with the same things I went through.

There are things I will talk about in this chapter that I still struggle with, but I think it is important to address these issues. I promise to be a hundred percent honest with my struggles in everything that I am going to discuss. I just ask that you keep an open mind and try to look past the things that you feel you don't want to hear to ask the Lord His thoughts on these ideas.

Sex and the media

Growing up in the south, the thing I heard more than anything concerning sex, drugs, alcohol, peer pressure, etc. was to "Just Say No!" which is great in theory. Until you enter a relationship and realize that just saying no is not as easy as it sounds because your body is designed to want to reproduce. I believe one of the biggest reasons for teenagers and young adults in the church having sex before they are married is because they are not given all the information.

As I mentioned in the first chapter, this was my story. All I had ever heard from the church is that sex was bad, and so I assumed that since it was bad, it would be easy to avoid. I was very wrong. I believe this saying also has many negative repercussions for when Christian couples get married. When all you hear for most of your life is that sex is bad and a sin, it can make your sex life in marriage suffer.

Instead of teaching that sex is bad, we need to be teaching that sex is sacred. And because it is sacred, we need to protect it. For example, imagine you have a bunch of teenagers over at your house one day and you have a priceless lamp passed down for generations on your nightstand. If all you say to them "do not break that lamp" odds are they won't be as careful around the lamp because they have no real understanding of why that lamp shouldn't be broken. However, if you tell them to be careful around the lamp and tell them a story of how it has been passed down in your family for generations and it is priceless, they will most likely be more careful around it because they understand the value behind it. Which is why I believe we see so many people in my generation and the generations below me losing their virginities at young ages. Because they do not understand the value behind it.

Sex is not bad. It is sacred. It was something that God put on this earth to be shared within the confines of marriage. Even in the past, the media at least showed sex as something you should do with someone you love, but it has grown past that. Now it is something that is just shown all the time and for absolutely no reason.

One of the biggest reasons we see so many issues with this generation and understanding the Biblical example of sex is because the media is setting the precedent for what sex is. Not the church. There are so many Christians that fall into sexual sin who love God with everything inside of them and carry so much guilt and shame because they fall into sin and feel like failures.

How are we supposed to avoid falling into sexual sin if no one talks about it until it is too late? A lot of what we do now as a church is damage control rather than preventative. We take the stance that we don't want to ruin the innocence of our children and teens, but reality is that it is being ruined way before we decide to talk about what it is. We talk about sex as though it is all a sin, and then suddenly you're married and BAM it's supposed to be good? This sets up so many mindsets that are detrimental in and out of marriage. The media has been setting the precedent for sex because they are willing to show sex while the church is not even willing to talk about it.

Bridgerton

The show that swept the nation during quarantine, with the love stories, the costumes, the dances, the wit. What is not to love about the show? One thing that I think this show exemplifies... not talking about sex has more repercussions than we think.

The main character in the first season is a young girl, Daphne, who is looking to get married. She falls in love with a duke who promised his father that he would never have a child. Because of some circumstances, the couple ends up having to get married. The Duke tells her he cannot have children, which she takes to mean that he physically cannot have a child. As she knows literally nothing about sex, she does not realize that what he meant is he is choosing not to have children. Since no one told her anything about sex, Daphne ends up in a horrible situation that is not romantic, but toxic.

What does this show teach us? Not talking about sex causes more problems than talking about it. If Daphne had just known one or two very basic things, her marriage would have started differently. Yes, now most of us know by the time we are that age how a baby is made, but there are also a lot more variables that go into our lives that make sex a greater temptation at a younger age, especially if we have no true knowledge of it.

I am not talking about knowledge of the act itself, but about everything else that goes into it. The emotions, the hormones, the fact that our bodies want to reproduce, etc. Teaching "Just Say No," I would argue never really has worked, but especially does not work in our current culture.

Teaching abstinence and telling kids not to have sex before marriage is obviously failing. I have heard many people who are older than I speak about how disappointed they are in our generation. How we have ruined so many things and are the generation that just sleeps around.

Think of it like this. If you are in a class and 90 percent of the class fails, it's not the class's fault. It's the teachers. I am not trying to push blame or make anyone feel bad. What I am trying to do is tell you we have to change the way we are teaching if we want to see a change in the outcome. We need to stop teaching that sex is bad unless you are married, and begin teaching what the Bible actually says about sex. Sex is Sacred. Sex is something that is meant to be shared within the confines of marriage.

When I was a senior in high school, my youth pastor did a series called "The Fire Within." It is a series that goes through love, dating, marriage, and sex. This series was the first time that I heard something helpful about what sex is. Unfortunately, I had already had sex by this point, but it was very beneficial to me when that relationship was over. I wish I had heard that years before, but I have no regrets where life has taken me. That being said, I wanted to share the two main things that impacted my view of love and sex from that series. He has spent years doing research on this topic, and I don't want to steal his work, but I want to share two things that I think everyone should know when it comes to love and sex. I hope that he eventually does a full recording of this series, but until then, here are the two big things that constantly impact my life from that series.

"The Fire Within" by Michael Christian

1. There are three types of love mentioned in Song Of Solomon concerning love.

   Rayah: *best friend love. Has nothing to do with romance*

   Ahava: *commitment. Says I am going to commit my life to you*

   Dod: *physical, erotic type of love, sexual love*

   > *It takes a combination of these three types of love to have a strong marriage that cannot be broken.*

2. There are neurochemicals that are released in our brain that create connections between other people. These chemicals are released during sex. Each of these chemicals are also "feel-good chemicals" which cause our bodies to want more of them.

The first is dopamine. This chemical is released any time you do something good your body enjoys. When you do something good, your body releases this chemical to tell you to do it again. Sex is one of the strongest generators of dopamine.

The next chemical is called oxytocin. Oxytocin is released in larger amounts in females. Oxytocin is a chemical that creates a bond with any physical connection, so it can go from holding hands to sex. This chemical also creates a bond for you with that other person. This is one reason girls get attached stronger in relationships. It is not all about emotions, but about a chemical bond to that person.

The last chemical is vasopressin, which is seen more heavily in males. Vasopressin has a lot of the same attributes as oxytocin, except vasopressin is released less and less with each new person. Therefore, the more a guy has sex with different people, they have less and less connection.

Those two points are the two things that I always have and always will remember about that sermon series. Here is a breakdown of why I remember them and what they mean in our lives.

Rayah, Dod and Ahava love

These three words always stick in my mind because it helps me to remember what I am looking for in my future marriage. When I start thinking about relationships, I know that these three things are the things I need in it. I want that best friend, committed and sexual love in my marriage. I think that too often in life we get caught up in just finding one of the three, and then decide it is okay to go on without the other two, but each part is just as significant as the next.

In a relationship, all three of those aspects need to be present. As a church, I believe we sometimes forget to put the same significance on the sexual aspect of a relationship as we do the best friend and committed side. I believe in our minds we make ourselves believe that the physical does not have to be at the same level, but those three types of love were meant to not only exist together but to grow at the same pace. What does that really mean for us? That the sexual side of a relationship matters.

Dopamine, Vasopressin, Oxytocin

I think the most important thing to take from this concept is that physical escalation in a relationship is natural. It isn't something to feel shame about, but rather a natural product of chemicals in our body. In order to have control over that, we have to understand how the chemicals and escalation work.

One thing that is rarely talked about in church is how relationships escalate. While your relationship could start innocently, it could morph into something you weren't expecting before you even realize it. In relationships, the physical aspect is just as important as the rest. What is important to realize is how our bodies respond to the physical side of a relationship. Your relationship may start with hand holding, which will start by feeling excited and releasing

135

chemicals into your brain, but the more often you do it, the less exciting it gets and the more your body will want something more. It is the normal escalation of a relationship, but if you don't recognize it, then it could escalate past a point that you are comfortable with.

For instance, this is how it might escalate from a female perspective. You start by holding hands, but then you want a little more, so his arm slips over your shoulder. From there you share a brief kiss, which eventually turns into a make-out session. Once you get used to that, your hands may start to wander and suddenly your shirt is off. From there, it could escalate to having your hands down each other's pants, to oral sex and eventually sex.

This timeline could look different for each couple. It could be in the span of days, weeks or months, but if you are not paying attention to it, then you cross a line you didn't think you would cross until you were married. That is how I have seen it happen to most people, including myself. It was a series of pushing little boundaries until I crossed the one that I had promised myself to wait to cross until marriage.

When it comes to sex, the church is oddly quiet about a lot of things. This is, of course, a generalization and not true for every church, but I am afraid that a lot of these things are true for most churches. This is not to say that if a church does not talk about these things, then it is a bad church. As I stated earlier in my testimony, my church did not thoroughly cover this topic for a while, and I wholeheartedly believe my church is an amazing, God-loving community. This is meant to show opportunities to grow, not for condemnations. What I have done is gone through typical stereotypes about sex and what the church says about them, what the Bible says and what the media says. I came up with this by having many very vulnerable conversations with friends about what they wish they would have known about sex growing up.

The media

- Sex is good and should be experienced
- It is okay to lose your morals if you love that person
- Sex is expected in any relationship

The church

- Sex is bad, unless you are married, then it is good
- Sex should not be talked about
- Sexual sin is a lack of self control
- No one will love you if you are "damaged"

The Bible

- Sex is sacred
- It was meant to as a gift to be experienced with your spouse
- It creates more intimacy in a relationship

A dilemma of contradictions

We are currently being taught two very drastic contradictions. On one end, we have the media telling us that sex isn't something very serious and should be enjoyed anytime, anywhere, with basically anyone you want. Then we have a good majority of church and sex education saying that sex is bad and we should avoid it at all costs until you are married. Both ends have swung to the extremes. I believe that the Biblical view of sex lies right in the middle. Sex is sacred and should be experienced in the confines of marriage, but it is no less beautiful.

It was always meant as a gift of intimacy. There is an entire book of the Bible (Song of Solomon) dedicated to the beauty of sex. But somehow we have created sex into a taboo topic that shouldn't even be talked about after you are married.

How do we manage our sex drives?

In college, I took a class that went through sex and relationships. One of the most memorable moments of the class was when she began talking about how unrealistic it is that we have an expectation of people to not have sex when we have given no information or tools to help them. She walked us through the science that I won't bore you with, but essentially it boiled down to the fact that most people's sex drives start when they are 12-13. The average American gets married between 27 and 29. That means there are over 10 years of having an active sex drive that we are expected to know how to control it with no tools being given to us. Worse than that, for the most part, people go through this battle alone. Even though we all go through the same things, we have been taught that it is something we do not talk about.

So we go into this battle alone and uninformed, and there is still an expectation of winning. We were not meant to fight this battle alone. Here are a few things that I have learned from my years of being single and having to learn how to fight this battle.

The battle of the mind

In my opinion, the most important step in winning this battle is to win the battle of your mind. Our bodies were designed to want sex, which means that our mind can have a tendency to think about it. I'm sure the battle in the mind has always been difficult for people but I think most people can agree that now is the hardest time in history to have complete control over your thoughts because we have things around every corner tempting us to let our minds wander.

How far is too far?

This may be one of the hardest and most frustrating questions to answer concerning this topic. I asked this question for years and never got actual lines to draw, just hypothetical theology. I have heard sermons where they say "just go to what makes you comfortable that you won't be tempted to have sex." But that leaves so much room for technicalities. I think it needs to be a conversation between you and the Holy Spirit, but as a general rule, I would say that all clothes need to stay on, and nothing goes underneath clothing.

A new era of porn

I promised complete honesty at the beginning of this chapter and right here is where you are going to get the most vulnerable, honest side of me. As I am writing this, I honestly don't want to be because it is a topic that for me I sometimes wish I felt differently, but I have been very convicted of this topic. This is something I still struggle with, and that I wrestle with constantly to find what the line is of what should be allowed into my mind when I am watching something.

It feels almost impossible to watch a good show where there isn't some form of sexual content. To be brutally honest with you, there are a good amount of times where I have watched a show and the sexual content came on that I enjoyed watching it. I didn't feel convicted or guilty because it's not porn, so what does it matter? The fact is, lust is lust. It doesn't matter if the content comes from Netflix or from PornHub, it is still lust. The only reason we don't see the shows we are watching as porn is because we labeled it as something that is okay. The definition of pornography is printed or visual material containing the explicit description or display of sexual organs or activity, intended to stimulate erotic rather than aesthetic or emotional feelings.

The definition of lust is to have a very strong sexual desire for someone.

You can label it whatever you want, but the fact remains the same. We have porn masquerading in our entertainment. When I first started processing this idea, everything inside of me wanted to deny it. I've watched Game of Thrones and Bridgerton, but I watch for the story lines so that's fine, right? Except that it's a lie.

I have definitely looked forward to the scenes where you get to see an attractive male take off his shirt. Or to see the romantic make out scene with my favorite couple. And I have hidden it and said that it doesn't matter because it's just a show, but lust is lust. If you are not lusting, it may be a different sin creeping up that we still ignore: coveting what is not ours. This is one that took me some time to wrestle with, again, because it is much easier to just say it's fine and move on.

But as a Christian, my goal is to try to see things the way Christ does and try to make my life look more like his. I used to think it couldn't be envy because they are not real people, but I would envy the relationships that I would see. We crave those relationships we see. It is a simple vocab switch to go from craving to envy. I see so many people who judge those who watch porn when they themselves watch shows that are just as bad. The only difference between the two is the mindset that one of them is okay and the other is not.

Do not fight the battle alone

If you get nothing else from any of what I am writing, I am begging you to get this concept. This applies not only to sex, it is with everything. Do not fight your battles alone. I believe it is one of the greatest strategies of the enemy, to divide and conquer. I fought this battle alone for years. I didn't realize the impact my thoughts could have on my day-to-day life, but more than that, I believed my friends would change their opinion of me if they knew that sometimes I struggled with the sexual side of being single.

At this moment, I have been single for almost seven years, and it wasn't until around the third or fourth year that I began to be honest with people about some of my struggles. You want to know what happened? I learned they were in the same boat. I learned that they also sometimes struggled with sexual urges, but felt alone because of how much shame they felt. Shame at something the body does naturally. My life

140

absolutely changed when I started being real with my female friends. Suddenly I didn't feel alone and ashamed, but I felt connected and able to fight the battle, because it is still a fight.

We are supposed to go against our bodies' natural design for years until we get married, which means that there are going to be some hard days. What's important to remember is that you do not need to feel shame for experiencing what your body was made to experience. Instead, create an open community where you can be real about your struggles so that you can help each other through it. The times in my life where I have noticed a significant decrease in this battle are when I am living in a healthy community with other people.

Chapter Eleven:

Love Story Or Lust Story?

A purity stolen

Media is stealing our purity. I do not just mean sexual purity; I mean every definition of the word. In the Blue Letter Bible (an online resource for studying the Bible), one way purity is defined is as being free from corrupt desire. Purity is not solely about sexual immorality. It is about your heart and mind and goes into every aspect of your life.

We are living in a day where our purity is being taken from us at younger and younger ages while we just sit around and do nothing. We see our television shows and social medias becoming more and more about sex and yet we either chose to turn a blind eye or turn straight to judgement. We don't need either of those things. What we need is a battle plan.

Purity is not just about sex. I recognize that biblical purity is not only about sexual immorality, but the part I want to focus on is sexual purity. I know that for some people out there, this is a touchy subject because not everyone has represented purity to our church culture in the way that it should. What I want to do is go through what I have learned about purity over the last few years. Before we get to that, I think we have to recognize how the church has previously portrayed purity and purity culture.

Does this sound familiar to you? Someone on stage is trying to represent purity and gives an example that goes something like this. A person stands on stage with a white paper heart. They tell you that every time you do something physical with someone, a little piece gets ripped off. They begin ripping a bunch of pieces off until there is only a small, messed up piece of paper and tell you it is what it looks like sleeping with someone before marriage. Or maybe it wasn't a piece of paper for you, maybe it was a water bottle that had dirt put into it, that symbolized having sex makes you dirty and no one wants to drink a glass of water with dirt in it.

Illustrations like this have caused so many people, myself included, to isolate themselves when they fall into sexual sin. To isolate because they feel as though it would be better to feel alone than to have people know that they "dirtied their heart." But from my experience with Christ, this could not be farther from the truth. Purity is not solely based on sex. If you have had sex before marriage, it does not mean there is a piece taken out of your heart. I do believe that having sex before marriage is a sin and does have an impact on your life, but it is not an irredeemable mark. From my time reading scripture one of the biggest things I have noticed is the Bible shows more on redemption of sexual impurity than it does prevention.

I am here to tell you it is not just about if you have had sex or not. There is so much more to it. To start, I want to share a little of my journey on this subject.

My purity journey

About halfway through my first semester of college, I was having lunch with my best friend. I had decided earlier that I was going to tell her that while I dated that boy in high school; we had slept together. It was something I had never told anyone else and was beyond scared to tell her. I was so afraid she would be disappointed in me. Instead, the first words that came out of her mouth were "how is your heart doing?" That was the last response that I had thought she would say, but it was everything that I needed to hear. It was those words that helped me to heal from something which I did not know I needed healing from and what started me on a journey of learning what purity is. At that point, I thought purity was something I could no longer achieve. Something that I lost the day I said yes. I have never been so wrong in my life and I am so thankful for that. I want to share with you what I learned while searching to understand purity.

Purity is more than the physical

We have toned down purity to where it is simply about a physical state because recognizing how complicated it is makes it harder for us to achieve. Making it about a physical state makes it something that is easier for people to judge. Recognizing it is more than physical, and more than sexual, means recognizing the daily effort to be pure. It's easy to justify certain thoughts or actions when you believe that purity is a simple question of whether or not you have had sex. Purity is so much deeper than that. It is about our hearts and minds.

Currently, the media is stealing our purity by telling us evil things are good and good things are evil. Telling us that stabbing someone in the back is okay if they deserved it. Or that it is okay to be a toxic person if other people pushed you to that point. Teaching us that not honoring your parents is okay as long as you are pretty sure you know best. It has caused our minds to not even recognize that we are being robbed of the purity that we are called to live in. If you don't believe me, look at the fact that most children see pornography for the first time in the second grade. If that doesn't tell you something is wrong, I do not know what will.

Purity is not a physical state, it is a spiritual one. You can have an impure mind and never have slept with someone. Which meant that just because I was no longer having sex, that didn't magically bring back my purity. What I would come to learn is that it goes so much deeper than the physical and goes into our hearts and our minds. Purity means controlling the thoughts I have when I find someone attractive. It means when a sex scene comes on television that I skip it in order to protect my mind and my heart. It means that when someone hurts me I control what I think and say about them.

We are in a time where maintaining purity is harder than it ever has been. Why? Because everywhere you look is sex. It's hard to stay pure in your mind when everywhere you look is a temptation to let your mind wander. We have this culture where so many people feel uncomfortable talking about things like this that we end up feeling unbelievably alone in our struggles. We feel as though we are the only ones going through things and that feeling only increases by the fact that as a church we have created a culture that says to "just say no" and puts no more discussion on things. This leaves people within the church who are struggling, feeling guilty, and alone. But we were always meant to have people around us who help us with things like this.

My friend Ayrial and I have been friends since we were in high school together. During this time we had a good relationship and I would say we both considered each other in our top friends list. Going into college, we kept our relationship, although we weren't as close since we were at different colleges. Flash forward a few years and I would consider her the person I am closest to. What changed?

We became more open with each other. We started having genuine conversations about things we were going through. I told her about some of my struggles that I had experienced in college with anxiety and feeling impure, along with so many other things. While her story is a lot different from mine, I would find out that she was going through very similar things while we were in college. We were going through the same things around the same times and both went through it alone because we were so afraid that the other person would see us differently or judge us for what we had done that we kept it

146

to ourselves. Which collectively led us to some of the loneliest moments of our lives.

It wasn't until about a year after her relationship was done and many years after mine that we finally opened up to each other about some things we had been through and were still dealing with. This ended up transforming our relationship into true Reyah love. A best friend love, being fully known by the other person. Now we have a friendship that truly is there for every aspect of life. When we are struggling or when we are thriving. That goes past the facade of what we want our lives to look like and goes into the nitty gritty of real life. All because we started talking about ways we struggled with purity in our pasts. It is not something to be ashamed of or feel guilty about, but something we need to have open conversations about. Otherwise, we will continue to see this idea of purity diminish more and more.

The battle of our thoughts

The struggle in our minds can sometimes be the hardest one because we are the only ones in our head. We don't put as much thought into our thoughts because other people will never know what is going on inside of it. Which then brings up the question: do you want to be pure, to be closer to Christ or to look good for other people? Trying to obtain purity with a performance base is impure in and of itself. Since we are the only people in our minds, we are the only ones with the ability to know when our mind is impure. No one can call us out on it or keep us accountable unless we are completely honest about where we are at. The thoughts in your mind are just as important as your actions.

Emotional porn

If pornography can create an unrealistic expectation of things in the brain, then how much more can television? PornHub released statistics that showed that most people spend an average of 10 minutes on their site when they visit. Most experts would agree that watching porn can have a negative impact on relationships and thoughts. Let's say that someone watches pornography daily. That is still significantly less time than the average person watches television. If that 10 minutes can impact the brain, how much more can hours of television impact our thoughts?

Does this sound familiar? You're laying in bed after watching a RomCom and all the sudden your mind wanders. You think about what it would be like if you had that guy in the movie. Maybe you even attribute some of the characters' aspects to someone you know. You make up a relationship in your mind of what it would be like if you had someone like that. Maybe the next time you see that cute person in your class you think "wow, what if he took me to a carnival and won me one of those cute teddy bears." Or maybe imagining what it would be like if you lived in Mystic Falls or on the upper east side. Our minds spend so much time creating these fake realities that we convince ourselves that those worlds would be better than ours.

I have heard the term emotional porn several times during sermons or talking to people, and it was a concept that took me a little time to get on board with. My initial thought was "well they shouldn't be compared because one is showing people having sex, the other is showing people fall in love." I thought through the idea behind the saying "emotional porn" and thought about how a big part of porn is that it creates lust in people. It causes people to crave sexual desire for the person they are viewing on screen, which caused me to view these shows that people thought of as emotional porn as emotional lust. Some could argue that a lot of movies and shows coming out are basically porn, but that is not the point I want to focus on. I want to focus on this idea that emotional lust comes up when seeing movies or tv shows that show people falling in love.

These shows and movies show us this picture perfect couple who look amazing and somehow are brought together even though in real life something like that probably won't happen. For example, Ross and Rachel, Damon and Elena,

Chuck and Blair, Allie and Noah, Peter Parker and MJ. It creates this image that we want badly. These images cause us to want that relationship, to yearn for it, even to become a little turned on by watching the show. The definition of lust is to have a very strong sexual desire for someone. These shows can cause us to lust after people because we crave emotion and that causes us to lust after that guy in the same way the physicality of pornography causes men to lust after women.

I recognize that women also struggle with porn and that there are probably a lot of men out there who can relate to what I am saying as well. I am not trying to say that these problems are gender specific, but I do think it is important to recognize the biological differences in men and women. I do believe that there are probably a lot of men out there that relate to the idea of emotional porn just as I know there are women who struggle with porn addictions.

Females and males work differently. Our anatomies were made to work differently. Men are more physical, while women tend to be more emotional. That does not mean that they don't have attributes of others, it means that we have differences. Sometimes we have more negative association with guys when we think about a guy thinking of sex, but ladies, when we create a relationship in our head with someone, we are not doing much better. We are also creating unrealistic expectations for men.

Expectations versus fantasies

An extremely important point that everyone needs to recognize is that I am not saying to not have expectations for the people you are dating. You should have expectations for people you date. The simplest way I can describe the difference is that expectations are characteristics while fantasies are scenarios you make in your mind. For instance, one of the attributes that my future husband has to have is being a man who chases God and can lead me in my walk with Christ. A fantasy would be thinking of what it might be like if the cute guy at church one day showed up with flowers and a string quartet.

Battle plan

If we want to have sexual purity in today's world, we have to have a plan. I am going to share with you my plan, but I encourage you to go with the Lord and see how you can make a plan that fits you.

Repentance

When you look at scripture, you can see that when it comes to sexual immorality, it talks about redemption more than prevention. Look at King David. A man after God's own heart. A man who famously slept with his neighbor's wife and then killed her husband. Yet he is still called a man after God's own heart. If that were a pastor today, I can all but guarantee he would have been fired and probably not listened to for years, if ever listened to again. We have put this standard on sexual immorality that almost makes it seem like an irredeemable sin. What we need to be doing is recognizing that God has used so many people who failed in this area. In the same way as David, when we fall short, we need to repent.

Repentance is what brings us closer to God and purifies our hearts and our minds. Repentance is not just saying "my bad, I'll try not to do it again." Repentance is going before God and spending time to change your heart and your mind.

It's not about suppression

I believe we struggle so much with inappropriate thoughts in this generation because we have been taught that suppression is key when we should teach on how to fight temptation. Suppressing feelings will only cause them to bottle up, and eventually cause an explosion that you cannot control. If we learn how to deal with temptation when those urges arise, we then have the ability to control what is happening.

Learn to control your thoughts

This is easy to say and much harder to implement. As I said earlier, your thoughts are the easiest thing to convince yourself are okay because you are the only person who knows them. In order to accomplish this, the want for betterment has to come from a relationship with God. If you only do it because I or someone else told you to, it won't stick. Doing it for performance only works for a short time. In order to sustain, you need a relationship. When your brain starts to plan your wedding with a guy you just saw in a coffee shop, open up your Bible and do some reading. If you start imagining what someone looks like naked, turn on some worship music. Train yourself to redirect your thoughts so you don't get mad at yourself when your mind wanders. You learn to redirect. Learn ways that work for you to connect with God. Find the way you connect with God and use that. It could be painting, dance, singing, journaling, the list truly goes on forever.

Set up accountability

This could look different for every person. For some people, it may be a person. For others, it may be having strict controls over what you watch. The important thing to do is to have a system that keeps you from temptation. For instance, there are programs out there that have controls so you can watch your favorite shows, but it will skip over sections you do not want to see. This takes away the temptation of you when you fast forward yourself because there are always those thoughts of "well I can just watch this one scene." If you have a program doing it for you, you can be held accountable at all times.

Do not fight alone

As I have stated so many times already, community is essential to our lives. Having people in your life who you can not only talk about these things with but can also go through them together can make your life a million times easier. It's when we go at it alone that we are more likely to fall into temptation. In order to do this, it takes an act of bravery to be the first person to open up. It takes courage to let part of your heart be open like that, but when you do, I can guarantee that both of your lives will be easier.

Use your strongest resource

Too often we fight this battle without friends, and without God. I know for me personally, there have been so many times in life where I am struggling with something and am ashamed to admit it to God and so I try to fight the battle on my own and neglect my strongest resource. In order to do this we need to utilize God's strength while recognizing His grace.

"For the grace of God has appeared that offers salvation to all people. It teaches us to say 'No' to ungodliness and worldly passions, and to live self-controlled, upright and Godly lives at the present age, while we wait for the blessed hope - the appearing of the glory of our great God and Savior, Jesus Christ, who gave himself for us to redeem us from all wickedness and to purify for himself a people that are his very own, eager to do what is good." Titus 2:11-12.

It is through God's grace and His strength that we become pure. Trying to do so without Him is like trying to swim across the ocean when a boat is right next to you. In order to win the battle and pursue purity, we need to invite the Holy Spirit into that journey.

Our purity is a gift that should be fought for. It is not something that we should be okay with throwing away for the sake of entertainment. We have to fight back. We are in a battle that most of us are unaware is being fought. It is really hard to win a battle that no one is fighting. I am convinced that when we wake up and start fighting the battle, we will realize the realness of what Christ has in store.

Where
Do We
Go From
Here?

There are two main things that I have hoped and prayed would be the outcome of this book.

1. For people to recognize the impact and influence media has on their life and to get people to think.

2. To think through the things I talked about that impact them and are relevant in their everyday life.

I recognize that there will have been parts of this book that some people relate to and some do not, but more than anything I hope people walk away and just think. As you read through the next few sections, I ask that you keep that in mind. If you read something you disagree with, I actually love that. I hope this made you ask questions and ponder different aspects of your life and media influence. I recommend you read every section as they each have something to offer.

A phrase that changed my life was "the difference between discipline and punishment is that punishment looks at your past and discipline looks toward your future." I was on a random school zoom call when one of my teachers dropped that piece of knowledge that changed my perspective on basically everything. So often in life when we want to change something in our lives we do it from a place of punishment. A place that says you haven't been doing a great job and because of that I am going to punish you for what you have been doing. Discipline looks to your future and says that because of where you want to go and who you are called to be, you need to make some lifestyle changes. This book is not meant for you to punish yourself, but for us to become more disciplined in living a lifestyle that brings glory to God.

Chapter Twelve:

Now What?

Now that we have gone through all of this information, what do we do? I recognize I covered a lot of different things and there is a lot you can do with it, but I wanted to give you some practical advice on where to go from here. These are things I try to do, and sometimes honestly still struggle with, but I have seen such a difference in every aspect of my life when I started changing the way I do media. If you could not tell up to now, one of my biggest goals is to be honest with you, so I will be completely honest with you in where I struggle in each of these categories.

Limit your time

To be honest with y'all, this is one I struggle with daily. Especially when writing this, there were so many days that I would have so much rather just turned on Netflix and binge watched my favorite show and put this on hold. Honestly, there were days it happened that way. What I tried my hardest to do was to set up parameters for when I could watch TV. That can look different for everybody, so here are a few ways to do that.

1. Set up a system that only allows for a certain amount of time watching television. I know many people who use this system with social media and it works really well for them. If you still live with your parents, have a conversation with them and see if you can come up with a time frame that you can both agree on. Hear me out, if your parents disagree with you, they are still your parents and deserve your respect, so at the end they will have the final say. That being said, I think it is really important for you to have your own say in how much you are watching. You just need to be sure you are looking at a healthy time frame, not one that sounds easiest.

2. Set up a time to be done watching, or a time that you can start watching. This is the system that I have been using to help me write this book. I am a huge night owl, and so a lot of days what would end up happening is I would get home, watch some TV after work, then 9pm would hit and I would think "well that's the end of the day, I'll just keep watching TV" and would get very little done. When I realized how much work I could get done at night, I switched things and decided I could watch TV until 8, and then would have to work on things. My productivity increased exponentially. If you are not a night owl, I recommend doing the opposite of me.

Something important to remember is to have grace for yourself. If you accidentally go over one day, don't beat yourself up. If you have had a really hard day, let yourself have some extra time. If you do this, though, be honest with yourself if you are tired and need rest or are just feeling lazy.

This is one of my biggest struggles. It is really easy for me to convince myself that it was a long day or that I am tired and end up watching television. However, once I got in the habit of pushing through that and limiting screen time five days of the week, I found I enjoyed what I was working on more and more. I have found that when I limit myself throughout the week; I do not have as much to get done on the weekends because I was productive during the week.

Turn on your analytical mind

When you watch a show, instead of just moving on, ask yourself: "What is being taught in this show?", "How could this be affecting my life?", "Am I watching this for entertainment or because I want it to be a part of my life?" Honestly, this one is easy for me because I love to analyze things. A simple way to do this would be to come up with a list of questions to ask yourself every once in a while when watching a show. Most likely, this will end up becoming something you don't even have to think about. It will just be natural. I think this is especially important when you are watching things with harder issues, such as drinking, drug use, or suicide. The thing I have prayed over most when writing this has been that it will help people open their eyes to things in their own lives. To not just take my experience as theirs, but to analyze their own life and how the media has been impacting it. For you, it might not be shows, it may be video games or social media having the biggest impact. What matters is recognizing the part it is playing in your life.

Limit what you are watching.

Genuine honesty, this one is extra hard for me. There are so many shows out there that have content that I dislike, but amazing storylines. For me, sexual content is the one thing that I feel convicted from the Holy Spirit to control on my screen. Drinking and other things do not really bother me, but the amount of sex that is shown in shows today is insane to me. Even more real talk, there are some moments where I enjoy seeing the sex scenes that come across. Usually that happens when I am feeling a little more insecure about being single or am feeling lonely, but the fact remains that it's content we should not be watching. Especially at a young age.

The older you get, I think you have more wiggle room to judge what is compromising and what is not compromising to you. It is important to invite the Holy Spirit into that conversation and not just base it on what you think. If I didn't invite the Holy Spirit into this conversation, I can guarantee my answers would be a lot different. It is because of my relationship with Christ that I want to make these changes. From that relationship is where everything should flow.

If there are certain shows you want to watch that have inappropriate content, look into getting some sort of guardian app or controls. I still love Bridgerton, and I have the ability to watch the show while still protecting my mind. This does not have to be something where you leave behind every show you have ever enjoyed. It is purely protecting your mind and heart when those shows have inappropriate content.

The truth about sex

As I said earlier in the book, I wish someone would have explained to me when I was younger about what sex actually is. In case you do not have anyone you feel comfortable having that conversation with, I want to give you a few more tips and information on sex. I highly encourage you to find someone you know you can trust to ask questions, as there is only so much I can cover in a book without having a relationship with everyone who will read this.

Every single person reading this book will have temptations. It is something every single one of our bodies goes through and it is not something to feel shameful about. It is something we need to be prepared for. Do not go into this battle alone. Have friends and mentors who you feel comfortable processing these things with and people you can call when you are unsure of things. Remember that you are not doing this because sex is bad, but because it is sacred and you want to experience the incredible act of intimacy with your spouse.

Sex outside of marriage can feel good. For a moment. But then it leaves you feeling very empty. If you have already crossed that line, don't worry. So did I. Remember that it does not define you and that it does not make you less loved. It does not mean you are impure or that you will struggle to find someone to love you. All of these were thoughts I had in my head after I had sex. If you are in the boat, please know that you are still loved. God is not mad at you. That does not mean there will not be struggles and heartaches at times, but healing will come when you hand it over to God.

Find community

If nothing else I say sticks with you, please hear this: community is essential to life. I know I talked a lot about this in an earlier chapter, but I briefly want to cover again why it is so important. More and more, we see people leaning away from the community. I think there are many reasons for this, the highest being that there are a million things to distract us from the fact that we are lonely. We need people who will be there for us and to just do life with. Find a way to be in community. Community does not mean having the biggest friend group, it means having a deep friend group.

For so much of my life, I let part of my identity be based on how many friends I had. If I walked into a room and did not feel like I had my group to go to, I felt so insecure. I would start to doubt everything about myself, all because I did not have a designated group of friends at a function. I have come to learn that it's not about having the most friends. It's not about having a friend group everywhere you go. It is about having people who are invested in your life that you are in constant relationship with.

One of the things I learned after moving across the country a few times is that creating community is hard. It is really hard when you are starting from scratch. What I have learned when I move to a new place is not to feel like a failure when I do not immediately have people to hang out with on Friday nights, but to start by finding one or two people with whom I have a connection with and can begin a friendship. I have found that while I may leave those cities with only a few friends; I know they are people I will keep in my life no matter where I move to.

Fall in love with scripture

If we want to see our lives be more influenced by God than by the world, then we have to change what we are putting into it. Starting with scripture. The Bible is often referred to as a sword, and people always say to have your sword on you, but what good is a sword if you do not know how to use it? The way a lot of us function right now is by only using the sword when we need it, and not in preparation. That would be like a soldier going to war with a sword and Googling a YouTube video before a fight. Could it work? Maybe. Are there better ways to be prepared? Absolutely.

There are a lot of situations where we have time to go back and research things in the Bible that we are struggling with, but there are also plenty of times where we need to be prepared. If you are in a conversation with someone about a certain topic in scripture, you need scriptural evidence to back up your claim.

My whole life growing up, I've never doubted that women could be in leadership. My church growing up held this belief, so I saw women in leadership at the church for most of my life. When I went on to ministry school, I was hit with the reality that there are many people out there who believe women should not be in leadership within the church. During that time, if someone had asked me why I believed that and where I saw it in scripture, I would have been at a loss. So I took a woman in ministry class that taught me why women can be in leadership. It went through all the verses that are most commonly brought up and showed the theological background to why it is okay. What's the point? The times where people question if I should be able to preach or not, I need to have my sword ready to use, not in my pocket, with no idea how I should use it.

Learning to love the word has been one of the longest journeys of my life. Growing up, I heard so many people always talk about what you "should do" with scripture and it had this stigma that doing things differently wasn't as holy. You may have heard something similar, so see if this sounds familiar. "You should start every day with time in your Bible, a short devotional, and some journaling. After that, you should probably pray for at least 30 minutes and then you can start your day." One thing to know about me, I hate mornings. I will sleep until the absolute last second I can before going somewhere. So this idea of having to do these things did not work for me. Instead, it created immense guilt.

While I was in high school, I would always hear girls around me talking about this type of routine that they had and as they talked, my guilt grew. "Am I a bad Christian because I do not do a morning devotional?" My guilt grew continuously. I never felt like I was doing the right thing. As the guilt grew, the less and less I wanted to read scripture until I was really only in scripture on Sundays and Wednesdays. I wanted to know more about God, but I thought reading scripture just wasn't for me. In college, I would go through phases where I would do really well at reading scripture and then would stop for a while and start feeling guilty again.

Even while I was in ministry school, I struggled to find a love for scripture. In my last year at school, I took a class called "Loving the Word" that spoke straight to my heart. I want to share with you some tips I learned from that class, along with some things I have noticed over the years. I hope these things can help you find a new love for scripture.

Get rid of guilt

If you are constantly feeling guilty about reading the word, you will never fall in love with the word. If you are only reading scripture so you feel like a "good Christian," then you will never truly fall in love with it. Reading scripture needs to come from a place of relationship, not performance.

Get rid of performance

I struggle with this like crazy. Most of the time when I felt guilty about not being in the word, a lot of that guilt came from feeling like other people were judging me. It wasn't about transforming my heart; it was about performing for people. In order to be transformed by scripture, you need to do it from a place of wanting to know more about God, not a place of wanting other people to see you as a good Christian.

Find a time you can read

As I mentioned, I am not a morning person, but I am a huge night owl. So now I do most of my intentional time with God in the evenings. I try to start my day with worship music and end it being intentional in the word. There is not a time that is more spiritual to be in scripture. I promise you every time of day has equal value.

Be in relationship

Scripture was always meant to be combined with relationships, not to just read empty words on a page. You can read scripture every day for hours and get absolutely nothing out of it. This was the problem with the Pharisees. They were so focused on the law that they could not recognize how a relationship with Jesus was what they were missing. Scripture should be combined with our relationship with Christ to get what we need out of it.

Go for quality, not quantity

It doesn't matter if you read the entire Bible if you got nothing out of it. We have to lose the performance mindset with scripture and go there to be fed. This could look like only reading a few verses a day, but meditating on those verses to get the most out of them. It is not a contest to see who can read the most scripture. The purpose should be to learn and be transformed.

Re-read scripture

Don't feel you have to have an exact understanding the first time you read it. Sometimes I can read an entire book of scripture and feel as though I only remember minor parts of it. I like to think about it like this.

Friends is my favorite show of all time. The first time I watched it, I could tell you the major plots, but that was about it. The second time through, I could tell you more of the plots of some episodes, but still mainly had a general understanding of the show. By the time I had watched it for the fifth or sixth time, I could tell you everything about it. I could say lines before the characters said them and I could tell you an episode's plot based on the name. Scripture is no different. The first time you read it, you may not have a full grasp on it, but the more you read it, the better understanding you get.

Read in community

This does not have to be a solo thing. It was only recently that scripture had such easy access. Before it was widely spread, it was only read by groups of people in the community. In order to get the fullness of scripture, you need to be discussing it with other people. This helps us to push our beliefs and challenges our viewpoints of things. If we only discuss scripture with people who have the same viewpoints as we do, then we miss the opportunity to learn more about who Christ is.

Take a break

I had to do this in order to fall in love with scripture. I took a break for about a month to not be in it daily (I still read it for church and what not) but I wanted to break off all the strings that I had in my head for reading scripture. Do not take this as an excuse to not be in scripture. This is purely for a short time, to be in prayer and conversation with God about how to renew your mind so that you love His word.

The next chapter is aimed towards parents, but I highly encourage you to read it as well. It should help give you some ideas on how to communicate with your parents or guardians about television. The last chapter is on the Church. Please read that chapter and know that every part of it is meant for the entire church. Not just people in ministry, it is meant for the body of Christ. No matter your age, if you believe in Jesus, you are a part of the church. This means that you have the ability to change culture within the church. I encourage you to read that chapter and ask yourself what it means in your life as a member of the church.

Chapter Thirteen:

For the Parents

I encourage everyone to read this section, not just parents. I am not a parent. I am not anywhere close to being a parent, and I do not want to tell you how to parent your child. However, I am not that far off from being a teenager and also have spent most of my adult life in some form of student ministry. These are students that I look at like my own family. All I want to do in this section is give you some advice from someone who grew up in a similar situation to today's youth, that will hopefully help you connect and grow with your children.

In a generation that has all the world's information at their fingertips, most of us crave one thing with rules: understanding. We like to know how and why things are a certain way. I recognize that as a parent, there needs to be a definite power hierarchy, and I am not asking you to compromise on what you believe is the right way to parent. However, I think there are some ways to help you create boundaries with your children that they will respect and follow.

Even now, at 25, I still want to understand why I am not allowed to do something. I was at the airport a few days ago and there was a sign when I was entering the plane that said:

"Do not touch." I wanted so badly to touch that sign because I wanted to know what it did. I wanted to know the reason I could not touch it. Was it dangerous or just breakable? Could it kill me? If it could kill me, then why is there only a small sign in front of it?

In the same way, every teenager and young adult I know just wants to understand why certain rules exist. Instead of only saying what they can and can't watch, open up a dialogue with them to ask what certain aspects of TV they think would be appropriate and not appropriate and ask them to explain why. Give your answer as well and start an open discussion as to what you both think is best. At the end, come up with a list of aspects that can or cannot be in shows they watch. For example:

Can:

- Language
- Moderate violence
- Moderate sexual content

Cannot:

- Graphic sexual content
- Nudity
- Extreme gore

After you have made your list, create a list of shows that fits into this. I believe this is important for movies as well, but we spend a far greater amount of time watching shows than movies. If you are wondering about certain shows, look up the parents guide to them and go through what it says for each section.

At the end of the day, your decision is the one that matters, but I fully believe that by opening up a conversation, you bring the opportunity for you both to grow. Let the conversation be filled with life giving things about values and what matters to each of you. Just make sure it is a two-sided conversation.

In the same way that giving a toddler choices helps reduce tantrums, giving teens input helps reduce angst. I believe that opening the dialogue will not only help you to come to an agreement but also helps prepare people for when they move out.

Use TV to bond

One reason I think I connect with students so easily is because I can talk about the things they are interested in. I can have a full conversation of why I am team Stefan or Damon, or about what I thought of the newest season of Outer Banks. If you show genuine excitement about what your child is watching, there is a good chance they will talk about it with you.

My senior year of high school, I started watching Once Upon a Time with my mom and it became our favorite thing to do together. I had a summer where I stayed with my Nana and we watched so many TV series, and I came out of it feeling extremely close with her. Television does not just have to be a place of argument, but can be a form of connection.

The birds and the bees

I am in no way an expert on how to have conversations with your kids about sex, but I have some knowledge that I can share with you that I learned in college. If you really want to dig deeper into this, there are plenty of resources out there that would give you a deeper look at this. My first recommendation: try your hardest to never make sex a taboo thing. If you get asked about sex, answer honestly and try your hardest to not make it awkward.

Make sure you introduce the topic before television does. In the next chapter, I will talk about how, as a church we need to be better about how we discuss sex, and I believe many of the same things are true in the home.

If your child watches a show or movie that has sex in it, talk about it. Do not make it a taboo subject that is averted anytime it is brought up because it feels uncomfortable. Teach them what scripture says about sex to help them learn about how God created sex, not how it has been transformed in today's culture.

Community

I have said it a bunch and I will say it again: community is essential. Let your kids have the ability to create community. When I was working in the youth ministry, I had an insane amount of conversations with students about how they weren't allowed to hang out with us after youth and really did not have much time to hang out with people their own age outside of school. Community is essential to our lives, and in order to do that, kids have to be allowed to hangout with people their own age outside of school and church.

Let your children have the opportunities to do things with their friends so that they can create a healthy community. It doesn't have to be out in public. Sometimes it can just be letting them bring a friend or two over one afternoon. Teenagers nowadays are under so much pressure and have so much going on. They need people their own age to help them through it. I look back at my time in high school and have no idea how I had the capacity to do everything that I was doing. One thing I remember above everything is the friends I had in my youth group. Many of those people are still my friends to this day. Our time together was not only Sundays and Wednesdays, but was movie nights, game nights, mission trips and going to eat after service. Those are the people who got me through high school and who I was so blessed to have. I cannot imagine what my life would have been like if I had not been able to be a part of that community. The people who would fall off of that group were the people whose parents would not let them do anything with us outside of youth.

Show them what a community should look like. People learn best from watching those around them. I recognize it gets harder as you get older, but community is essential to your life as well. My parents always tell me they made it through a lot of life because they always had their community. It was nothing huge, just a few families in the same stage of life who ended up being a second family to me. Because my parents modeled that so well, I have been able to mimic that in my life as well.

Chapter Fourteen:

The Church

We are called to be in the world, not of the world. In order to be in the world, we have to recognize what is in the world. In today's culture, there are a billion things telling us who we should be or how we act. Things that shape who we are. As a church, it is our job to show people who Christ is and how He can impact their lives and their stories.

We are supposed to be trailblazers, but have become people who just try to put out fires. We are meant to be setting the precedent for things, but we are following what the world sets. We are called to be bold, courageous, loving, and so many other things, but a vast majority end up sitting on the sidelines. Church was never meant to be a Sunday thing. It is meant to be a relationship that transforms every aspect of our life, yet we see many Christians who will criticize the local church but are unwilling to do anything about it.

We hold preachers and staff to higher standards than ourselves, pretending like there are different levels of holiness you have to obtain if you want to be in leadership, when every Christian should hold themselves to the same standards they hold their leaders.

It is easier to criticize than to do. One reason I truly did not want to go into ministry when I was younger was because from where I stood, it looked like a thankless job full of people getting mad at you for doing things that they also did. When I was called to ministry, I recognized things in the church that needed change and honestly, it scared me to want to bring it up because I was so afraid of being "canceled." I was not afraid of being canceled by the world. I was afraid of being canceled by other Christians.

I am not here to criticize or push blame. My only goal is to bring recognition that there are things that need to change. Everything that I just mentioned are things that I have struggled with and sometimes continue to struggle with. But at the end of the day, all I can do is try to live the life Christ called me to, and right now I feel the Lord putting it on my heart to talk about how the Church needs to address these topics.

In many churches that I have been to or seen, there is always some recognition that these things are a problem, but most of them focus on the news media. My goal in this chapter is to give suggestions on how we, as the church, can create culture instead of following it. Again, I do not wish to place blame, I only wish to share what I have felt the Lord lay on my heart for how we can effectively tackle the problem that is media. The most important aspect that I believe the church needs to tackle in a more effective way is sex and purity.

Sex and purity

In the 1960s, a social experiment was done by Gordon Stephenson. In this experiment, five monkeys were put in a cage with a ladder in the middle. On top of that ladder was a banana. When one monkey would go for the banana, all five of them would be sprayed with water. This continued until none of the monkeys would go for the banana. Eventually, the conductors of the experiment took out one of the original monkeys and replaced it with a new one. When the new monkey would go for the banana, the original monkeys would attack it, so they would not be sprayed with water. After a while, the new monkey also stopped. They then continued to replace the monkeys. Each time one was replaced, the new one would go for the banana and the others would attack it. Eventually, it was only new monkeys. Water had not been sprayed since round one, but none of the monkeys would go for the banana. It got to the point where none of the monkeys knew why they were attacking, they just did. The circumstances changed. The custom did not.

Today, we do the same thing with sex in the church. We do not talk about it, because we haven't been talking about it. Now there are additional factors regarding sex education, but yet most churches and schools stick to the same tradition of not giving information. Because of this, we have left the education of sex to the media. The media now sets the precedent for sex. It is where most kids learn about sex and form opinions about it. Now there is so much information out there, we can no longer afford to continue on the path of tradition when the circumstances have changed this drastically.

By the second grade, most boys are exposed to pornography. TV shows and movies show sex (or insinuate sex) constantly. But yet as a church, we stick with just saying abstinence is key. I said earlier in the book that sometimes we say something is unrealistic when it is actually just inconvenient. This is not the case here. Not talking about sex and expecting teenagers or young adults to "just say no" is purely unrealistic.

We cannot afford to continue to not talk about sex. Otherwise, we will have many more with a story like mine. Of a girl who wanted so badly to keep herself for marriage, but was not fully prepared for what a physical relationship looks like. There are many people who could read this and think "well her parents should have done a better job." I have a lot of friends who do blame their parents for losing their virginity. Honestly, my parents would have talked if I had asked questions, but as most teens experience, there is a time in your life where you do not want to ask your parents these questions. This is why, as a church, we have to step up and be the safe place where people can come to ask questions.

How do we talk about sex?

I recognize it's easy to point out issues and much harder to give solutions, so my goal is to give you all the advice I can think of that I think could benefit the teenagers in your church. This part in particular I spent an enormous amount of prayer and consideration on because it is probably one of the most debated topics of what to talk about and when. Here are a few things that I believe are important to have in any youth group.

Openness

If you want students and young adults to come to you with questions, then you need to be sure you have an atmosphere of openness. An atmosphere that does not prompt guilt and shame, but redemption. Scripture talks more about redeeming sexual impurity than it does prevention, so we need to be sure we have an atmosphere that lets people know there is no judgement for anything they have done. There is redemption. If you want students to come to you with questions, you may have to open the conversation. If someone has a question, don't make them feel bad about it or tell them it is not appropriate. Odds are, if you do not answer it, they will find another way to have it answered.

This is something that is easy to say, but harder to implement. It is easy to tell people that you have a safe space, but harder to take a genuine look at your congregation to see if that is true. Do you have a culture that promotes discussing hard questions? Do you leave room for real discussion and don't just tell people what they should believe? What is your response when someone in leadership admits to you they are struggling with a sin? These are all questions that we should ask ourselves about the environment we create around us. It is vital to create a safe space for younger people to come in to ask questions and have discussions so that they do not have to find outside sources to answer the questions for them.

Asking questions comes with a relationship. When I was interning for my youth group, people started asking me questions after I established a relationship with them. You cannot expect to walk into your youth room and have students come to you with questions they do not know how to ask. You have to establish a relationship in order to let them know you are a safe place.

Teach on sex

I think one problem we run into is that we always make sex this special topic or event that is only addressed going into a certain grade. If that is the only time you ever talk about sex, it is very unrealistic to expect students to understand in the way we expect them to. I am not saying to not do events on the topic. As I said earlier, my youth pastors series "The Fire Within" changed my life and it was an event. But it was not the only time we talked about sex. If people had questions, they would be answered. Don't make it a topic that is only talked about once every few years. It needs to be discussed regularly to not feel like a taboo topic.

I think the most important thing we have to do is make sure sex is not a taboo topic. We can sit here and say all we want that we create an open environment, but truthfully, how can we expect students and young adults to come to us with questions when a lot pastors can't even say the word sex in a sermon without making it uncomfortable.

The difference between sex and purity

Growing up, I did not understand the difference between these two things. I thought if you had sex; you were impure and if you didn't have sex; you were pure. I came to learn that the two are not mutually exclusive. You can be abstaining from sex and not have a pure heart. You can look through my section on my journey with learning about having a pure heart and how it helped to heal me. I think it is so important to teach this concept to kids as soon as possible.

Push community

I promise this is the last time I will say this (in this book). We need community. Which means that as a church we need to teach and push for a community. One trend that I have seen, and makes me very sad, is people moving away from community. Moving to strictly online church and nothing more. We were created to do life and ministry together, and that is when the church is at its strongest. When it is unified. If we continue to see this trend of people only watching one service online and then going on with their week, I believe we will see the percentage of anxiety and depression increase rapidly. I was set free from anxiety, but the things that keep me from going back to that space are my continued relationship with Christ and my community.

Utilize media

It amazes me that we have so much technology to take advantage of, but we just stick to using fog machines and crazy light shows. There is so much out there to help bring people in and help them create a relationship with Christ. Especially if you are doing youth or young adult ministry. It doesn't even have to be extravagant. It can be something as simple as creating a TikTok and having kids doing fun 30 second Bible stories to help get kids involved and invested in what you are doing. You can also resource other tools ministries are putting out.

I have said it once and I will say it many more times; The Chosen is an amazing resource to use. You could start a Bible study off of it or so many other things because the fact is, this generation is a generation that enjoys being entertained. While I believe that there is a balance for that (we definitely should not have people coming to church purely for entertainment). I feel like we have gone to the other side of the pendulum and try to use as few sources of media as possible and call it "unbiblical" when people have too good of a time in church. It is so important for us to recognize the technology being used in the world, and use it to create our own culture.

If we want to see a revival in the American church, which I would say most people do, we have to recognize how the media is influencing our culture. We cannot afford to sit back and wait until things hit the fan to start worrying about it. We should be at the front of the pack utilizing this new era of technology instead of pretending like it doesn't exist.

Generations

I think one of the most important things we can do right now as a church is to find a way to bring the generations together. There is so much division between every generation, but the Bible pretty clearly states that we need each other. In Acts 2, it says that all believers were of one mind. Not the older generation had one mind. Not the denominations had one mind. But all believers were of one mind. We were never meant to be a divided religion – not by age, not by ethnicity, not by denomination.

How can you bridge the divide? Set up systems for people to be in connection with people from other generations. As a generation, I think it is assumed that we do not want the input of generations before us, but that could not be farther from the truth. There is a vast majority of my generation that loves to learn and be in relationships with those older than us. We want to learn from and be loved by people who came before us. The problem that I have found in most of these situations is that usually the conversation ends up being very one sided. A lot of times, it ends up where we are being told what we are doing wrong or how we can be "better" and usually leaves us feeling like a terrible generation.

The relationships I have had with people older than me that have really thrived and molded me into who I am now all have one simple thing in common. They listen to what I have to say. They want to hear about what's going on in my life, how I am doing with things, what my thoughts are. It is because of them being truly invested in me that I listen to their opinions.

The thing that separates the people who have entered my life in a mentoring relationship and those that have not is purely that there are many people who want to express their opinion of my life without actually knowing anything about it. I have sat in sermons where my generation is just really crapped on, and it is usually very obvious to me that whoever is speaking has never attempted to have a genuine relationship with someone in my generation.

We long to be mentored. We long to have those who have gone before us pour into our lives, not to tell us what we are doing wrong, but to be fully invested in our lives. Once we see a person cares about who we are, we are willing to listen and give real thought into what is being told to us, but so many people just want to give their opinion (This is true in every generation.)

If you want to see the generational gap break, start by doing this one simple thing. Look for deep influence not wide. Find one person younger than you and really pursue discipling them. Meet with them, hear about their life, listen to their problems, and don't judge what they went through because it is not the same as what you did. Find just one person and see how you can be in their lives. It doesn't matter how old you are, just find someone who is younger than you and find a way to pour into their lives and see how the relationship changes not only them, but I can guarantee you will see some benefits in your own life as well. I have so many people who have taken the time to pour into my life, and it is because of those people that I am where I am today.

Unity

"If your beliefs cause you to carry a sword intending to slay people instead of a towel intended to serve people, then you might want to check your beliefs." -Nathan Teeters

As a church, we have to be unified. A house divided cannot stand. If I had to describe the American church, it would be divided. I feel like as Christians we spend a vast majority of our time trying to defend ourselves to other Christians instead of trying to share the Gospel. I believe in checking for false teachers. I do not believe that just because someone has a different theology than you makes them a false teacher or prophet. I went from a methodist/nondenominational church to a charismatic ministry school and one thing became very clear to me. The most hate comes from people of other denominations. We have to work on that. We have to stop this culture that writes off an entire denomination because they do church differently.

Throughout highschool, I was a part of my school's swim team. My swim team was a little different though. All the schools in our district trained together. We had one pool that we all trained at. One thing that I am so thankful for is the way my coach taught us to compete. Yes, we were competitors, but he did something that I think is very rare. He made four competing schools a family. The older I get, the more appreciation I have for that. When I was in the program, I didn't realize how special it was because to us it was just the way things were. Rather than hating the people that should have been considered our main competition, they were our closest friends. When we competed in relays or events against the other schools, we would go for our own schools, but if someone from our hometown was in the water, we were cheering for them.

That is what I believe the church needs to look like. Even though someone is a different denomination and has some different theology, we should recognize that they are a part of our team. I find it absolutely ridiculous that Christians spend most of their time defending themselves to other Christians. Instead, I believe we need to recognize that yes we may have different beliefs and different church preferences but we are all a part of the bigger team. We are all a part of the Bride of Christ.

We have to come together and fight the things that are coming against us. Too often, we get caught up in fighting other churches or other people within our own church. Unity is what we need.

Final Thoughts

God is the ultimate storyteller, but we have to be willing to hand over the script. In our world, there are so many things that are influencing our lives. The important thing now is to recognize those things. For some people, it may be social media, video games, television, news media, etc. The list goes on and on. We have to open up the conversation to be talking about these things. We need to recognize the narratives that are influencing our lives. Once we do that, we can finally start taking back the narrative.

"For the testimony of Jesus is the spirit of prophecy." Revelation 19:10. In other words, the things Jesus has done in someone's life He can do in yours too. The testimony of how Jesus worked in my life can be a prophetic declaration in your own life.

These are the things that were influencing my own life story. Recognition is the first step, taking action is the second. This is my story. Now tell me, what is shaping yours? It is time to take back the narrative.

CPSIA information can be obtained
at www.ICGtesting.com
Printed in the USA
BVHW031515161022
649504BV00006B/12

9 781945 423451